WELCOME, THINNER CITY

Urban Survival in the 1990s

Colin Ward is a writer whose books tend to explore popular and unofficial uses of the environment. They include *Arcadia for All* and *Goodnight Campers*, both written with Dennis Hardy, and *The Allotment*, written with David Crouch, as well as his well-known books on *The Child in the City* and *The Child in the Country*.

He won the Angel Literary Award for non-fiction in 1985 and was given the first Charles Douglas-Home Memorial Trust Award to write *Welcome, Thinner City*.

WELCOME, THINNER CITY

Urban Survival in the 1990s

Colin Ward

Bedford Square Press

Published by
BEDFORD SQUARE PRESS of the
National Council for Voluntary Organisations
26 Bedford Square, London WC1B 3HU

First published 1989
Copyright © Colin Ward, 1989

Typeset by AKM Associates (UK) Ltd, Southall, London
Printed and bound in Great Britain at
The Camelot Press Ltd, Southampton

British Library Cataloguing in Publication Data
Ward, Colin
   Welcome, thinner city: urban survival in the 1990s –
   (Society Today)
   1. Cities. Central areas. Environment planning. Proposals.
   I. Title II. Series
   711'.4

ISBN 0-7199-1252-0

Contents

Acknowledgements

This book is the outcome of the first Charles Douglas-Home Memorial Trust Award, instituted by his friends to commemorate Charles Douglas-Home, editor of *The Times* from 1982 until his death in 1985.

Their first award was for research into the revival of Britain's inner cities. As the recipient I was enabled to travel throughout Britain, as well as to Italy and the United States, and was given the opportunity to explore and reflect upon inner city issues.

Consequently, I am profoundly grateful to the Trustees and I have to state that just as they have in no way sought to influence my findings, so they can in no way be associated with any opinions expressed in this book.

I need to make the same expression of gratitude, with the same disclaimer on their behalf, to all those people who have helped me by sharing their own findings and conclusions with me. To mention only those in Britain, I must name among so many, Jacquelin Burgess, Derek Diamond, David Donnison, Anthony Fyson, David Hall, Peter Hall, Dennis Hardy, Michael Hebbert, John Macnicol, Ray Pahl, Alison Ravetz, Paul Thompson, Louanne Tranchell, John Turner and George West.

It has been a privilege to meet so many inner city residents who have worked against incredible discouragements to change their city and that of their neighbours. Without asking their permission, I dedicate this book to Thelma and Billy Floyd, of Liverpool 8.

Introduction

I enjoy cities. I was a city dweller for half a century and I have a fragmentary working knowledge of a dozen British cities. Consequently, I know how little I know and that it would take several lifetimes to understand them really well. I have, however, learned several things about cities.

The first is that the city is the common property of its inhabitants. It is, in the economic sense, a public good. But how can I say this when it is all too evident that it does not belong to them? Simply because the astronomical value given to central city land arises solely from the fact that it is at the hub of the activities of millions of people. *They*, not the owners, have created these values, which self-evidently belong to the citizens. The second is that some city dwellers are adept at making the city work for them: they know how to use the place where they live. It is equally obvious that there is a level of poverty and despair below which this urban wisdom is suppressed. But the third thing I have learned is that, except for the very rich, the very poor and the transients, whether tourists or dossers, the city as a separate physical entity no longer exists: it is just the centre of a network of communications. Quite apart from the fact that most British or American urban dwellers live in suburbs, you can today live in a remote village but work, play or even go to school in Newcastle upon Tyne, Cardiff or Bristol, let alone London. Similarly, you can live in the central city, but spend your day in any one of a number of sub-centres, or you can orbit between various sub-centres around the city, which thus loses the temporary importance it had before the industrial revolution was overtaken by the communications revolution.

The best faculty anyone can bring to the understanding of the problems of Britain's industrial cities is a sense of history. In the mid-nineteenth century they grew at a pace previously unknown and generated enormous wealth in a climate of free-market economic liberalism. The resulting squalor and misery was described by the novelists of the period: Disraeli's *Sybil, or the Two Nations*, Elizabeth Gaskell's *North and South*, Dickens's *Hard Times*. The accidental occurrence that symbolised a change in the national mood was the death of the Prince Consort from typhoid fever in 1861. Public health was at last seen as a matter for public intervention, and the notion that it was a sinful interference with the course of nature for public authorities to protect the citizens from polluted water, adulterated food and open sewers, was slowly abandoned. We entered a period of public regulation, municipal activity and enterprise. The grandeur of ·a dozen Victorian city halls up and down the country is a testament to this civic pride.

If the death of Prince Albert was the accidental signal of a change in Victorian attitudes to the problems of the city, the twentieth-century symbol of a change of mood was the collapse of a block of municipal flats, Ronan Point, as a result of a gas explosion in 1968. It brought to the surface growing misgivings and disillusionment about housing policies undertaken by city governments (albeit in pursuit of central government policies). The nation moved into a period of the curtailment of public investment in the cities. 'The party's over', a Labour secretary of state warned local authorities in the 1970s, and in the 1980s government consciously returned to the early nineteenth-century belief in the sanctity of market forces, and consequently a policy of the abandonment of public regulation, services and spending, a contraction of municipal activity and, inevitably, of civic pride, since the freedom of action of local authorities has been circumscribed almost out of existence.

This change in the public mood coincided with an unprecedented collapse of the economic basis in manufacturing industry in British industrial cities. The same change in mood and policy was accompanied by the same collapse of traditional industries in the United States. The authors of a comparative, statistical study of the relations between central government and the economy of cities, provide a mordant comment on the abandonment of the idea of the city as a public good:

In a functional sense the survival of modern cities is dependent on continued public regulation, services and spending. That is, there is some lower threshold of public provision below which people will no longer be willing or able to live in cities. There is no way of saying where that threshold is in the abstract: it has already been passed for many of the hundreds of thousands of people who have migrated away from the centres of old industrial cities. There is no contemporary precedent, nor any fully documented historical ones, to tell us what is likely to happen after all those who can leave have done so, leaving such cities populated only by a dependent underclass. The triumph of market forces will be complete when the last emigrants from Toxteth and the East Bronx pause on their way out, not to turn out the lights, but to strip the crumbling buildings of light fixtures and wiring for sale as scrap.[1]

There is a vital postscript to be added to this accurate prediction of the results of leaving the cities to market forces. In both the inner city districts singled out for comment above, local action by poor city dwellers has shown that it *is* possible to stem the tide of dereliction and despair (see Chapters 7 and 10). It is also evident from the experience of American and British cities that the current belief in market-led urban revitalisation is misplaced since it actually worsens the situation of low-income people, who are, quite simply, driven out of the market.

It might be comforting to suggest that there is a pendulum in public policy towards the cities, and that excesses of governmental paternalism are naturally followed by an excessive reliance on market forces. An inevitable swing-back cancels out the zealotry of left or right. But to the detached observer it is evident that governments of both ruling parties since 1945 have switched from one urban policy to another overnight, not through ideology but because they have been unable or unwilling to understand the historical and geographical processes at work in the city. As one insider remarks:

Either there is too little money to spend or too much. Sometimes Ministers will want to be seen to be doing something about inner cities, money suddenly becomes available, and must be spent as soon as possible. This means that I have sometimes been called to an urgent meeting at 11 o'clock having been given the papers at 10.58 with the instruction to 'do something' or 'get projects going'. This inevitably leads at best to a process-saturated approach to policy-making, or at worst to tokenism.[2]

Yet we have had a whole series of intelligent and imaginative watchers of the rise and decline of cities, with solutions ready at hand, from Ebenezer Howard, Peter Kropotkin, Raymond Unwin and

Frederic Osborn onwards.[3] One of these neglected sages, Patrick Geddes, remarked 70 years ago, in the context of Indian rather than of British cities: 'I have to remind all concerned, first that the essential need of a house and family is *room*, and secondly that the essential improvement of a house and family is *more room*.'[4]

Neglect of this elementary fact led to immense sums of money being spent in the postwar decades on doing the wrong things in cities. Britain has a long tradition of advocacy of dispersal, urging that we should use the natural outward movement of population from the overcrowded cities to lower the valuation of city land and thus make possible low-density city living. Sometimes this tradition has been adopted as government policy, but has then been the victim of a lurch of policy in the opposite direction. In 1989, for example, London's crisis was suddenly perceived in terms of endless traffic jams in the streets, dangerous overcrowding of suburban train routes and the fact that the number of annual passenger journeys in the London Underground alone had increased in the previous five years from 500 million to 800 million. How many of the commentators on the problems of getting around London related this 'terminal seizure' to the closure, years earlier, of the Location of Offices Bureau which from 1963 onwards had 'enormously facilitated' the outward movement of office jobs from central London?[5]

This book is a simple and modest contribution to the decentralist tradition. It urges that the problems of urban decay and regeneration are problems for the poor minority of city dwellers who get left out of policy decisions. My argument is that they should be enabled to create their own solutions, but that, inevitably, this enabling has to be a matter of public policy. I do not trust government, but neither do I trust market forces. My position is precisely that of John Turner, the advocate of dweller-control as the first principle of housing in the cities of the poor world: 'While local control over necessarily diverse personal and local goods and services – such as housing – is essential, local control depends on personal and local access to resources which only central government can guarantee.'[6]

In Chapter 1, I attack the idea that the cities have declined from some golden age and argue that such a golden age of British cities never existed. In Chapter 2, I evoke the legacy of the nineteenth-century prophets of the twentieth-century patterns of human settlements, and in Chapter 3 point to the fact that land speculation has destroyed the functions for which cities arose in the first place. Chapter 4 then argues that the urban poor are, in fact, trapped in the city, whatever their own inclinations. In Chapter 5, I go on to examine the 'task force' ideology of government support for urban renewal, while Chapter 6 looks at two of these initiatives in practice: the Glasgow Eastern Renewal (GEAR) in Glasgow and the London Docklands Development Corporation (LDDC) in London. My experiences as an innocent abroad, wandering around American cities, are described in Chapter 7. Chapter 8 is about our suspect rediscovery of an urban 'underclass', and the story of one successful attempt to permit low-income people to live in their own housing in the heart of their own city is related in Chapter 9. This theme is continued in Chapter 10 with half-a-dozen examples of residents taking control of their own homes in British cities. In Chapter 11, I attempt to draw lessons about the future of manufacturing industry in cities from the remarkable Italian experience. Chapter 12 insists that the 'greening of the cities' is not an optional extra but an essential of city survival. Finally, in Chapter 13, I attempt to list some of the essential city issues that ought to engage citizens, whatever their political preconceptions.

This book supports no party and no programme and is addressed to citizens of all parties and none, since an understanding of the issues involved in the crisis of the cities is a prerequisite of citizenship.

CHAPTER 1

THE ELUSIVE GOLDEN AGE

Every city had its golden age. But the golden age of any particular city is exactly like the arcadia of rural mythology: it was some unspecified time in the past before everything went wrong. When we talk about the decline of the cities we seldom describe the golden age they were declining from. And when we use words like renewal, regeneration or revitalisation (the language changes in every decade) we imply a state of grace from which cities have unaccountably fallen.

The most remarkable account of a city before its fall from grace was provided by Daniel Defoe in his *Tour thro' the Whole Island of Great Britain*, first published in 1727. He gave a vivid account of one British metropolis:

> It is a large stately and well-built city, standing on a plain in a manner four-square, and the five principal streets are the fairest for breadth, and the finest built I have ever seen in one city together. The houses are all of stone, and generally uniform in height as well as in front. The lower stories (of those near the Cross) for the most part, stand on vast square Doric columns with arches which open into the shops, adding to the strength as well as beauty of the building. In a word, 'tis one of the cleanest, most beautiful and best built cities in Great Britain.

Defoe's praise for Glasgow in the early eighteenth century provides an ironic contrast with the actual experience of that city in the subsequent 250 years. Yet we can already see the signs that his description of 1727 could be recognisable once again in 2027. That city has been transforming itself ever since the Second World War, with many a devastating error in policy, at a huge financial cost and at an even greater human cost.

The industrial revolution transformed some cities in one brief century of the history of urban civilisation and we are still struggling to cope with its consequences. It was, for the cities of Europe and North America, a tornado which swept through in the nineteenth century and has now dispersed, leaving us at the end of the twentieth century clearing up the debris and comforting the dispossessed. Those cities which were hardest hit by the incredible growth of industry and commerce in one century are those which are suffering most in the aftermath. We are reverting to a pre-industrial pattern of settlement and work. Cities, like Norwich, which were outside the path of the hurricane of industrialisation, prosper most today. Others, like Glasgow or Liverpool, were the hardest hit by the end of empire, the decline of British maritime supremacy and the footloose nature of modern capital.[1] Small industrial centres are growing, the big ones are dying. The victims get blamed, but the same weather report comes from the cities of France, Germany or the United States.

It was in Glasgow that I learned not only that all cities are different, but also that there are huge differences in people's experience of the same city. I first arrived there in 1943 as an 18-year-old conscript in uniform, and as soon as I clambered out of the former St Enoch's Station I was besieged by a horde of little barefoot boys crying 'Gie's a penny, soldier!' It was my first reminder that the golden age of the cities was always a long time ago. For this was the time when Glasgow's biggest employer, the Parkhead Forge and its ancillaries, founded by Napier and Beardmore in the nineteenth century and producing every variety of steel and, at one time, every conceivable steel product, including armour-plated warships, locomotives, even London taxi-cabs, was enjoying its final triumphs of imperial and military productivity.[2]

Full employment had been brought to Glasgow at last, yet all around were signs of extreme poverty and deprivation. The most important lesson that I failed to learn in 1943 was that the fruits of industrial success are so ill-distributed that they exist side by side with incredible deprivation. I know from personal experience that the city's golden age was not the Second World War, but we can go back to the First World War and find an exactly similar situation. Thus a modern historian writes:

The fortunes of the east end were linked with those of the empire. In the period of rearmament before the world war which was waged in defence of Britain's imperial position, the industries of the Clyde were booming and none more so than those of this

area. Nevertheless, huge numbers of east enders remained
trapped in poverty and in brutal housing conditions. By 1914,
there were no less than 700,000 people – roughly the present
population of the whole city – living in three square miles,
making Glasgow the most heavily populated central area in
Europe. The labour force was packed into its heart. In 1917,
there were more than four persons per room in 11 per cent of
Glasgow's houses, over three persons in 28 per cent and over two
in 56 per cent . . . the efforts of the City Improvement Trust had
been overtaken by natural population growth and the immigration of impoverished Highlanders and Irishmen many of whom
found the combination of work and crowded tenements to be an
improvement on their conditions at home. Co-existing with
these horrendous living conditions was a flourishing economy
which was expanding and diversifying.[3]

It was in fact neither expanding nor diversifying enough, and in
search of Glasgow's golden age we could go back to the mid-
nineteenth century, only to learn the impressions of a contemporary
traveller commenting that 'I have seen human degradation in some of
its worst phases, both in England and abroad, but I can advisedly say
that I did not believe until I visited the wynds of Glasgow that so large
an amount of filth, crime, misery and disease existed in one spot in
any civilised country.'[4]

The golden age of industrial Glasgow never actually existed. When
I was first there I was billeted not in Maryhill Barracks but in a
requisitioned house in Park Terrace, to my eyes incredibly grand and
spacious. Among the army bunks and folding tables and chairs that
so incongruously filled it, I could push aside the black-out curtains
from the vast plate-glass windows, and see the whole panorama of the
soot-encrusted city under its pall of smoke: the docks, foundries and
steel fabrication yards, the miles of grim, packed tenements. I
learned, just through living in Park Terrace, that the city also had a
large and prosperous middle class living in considerable splendour,
with the landscape of poverty visible beyond the trees of Kelvingrove
Park. For in those very years, the last gasp of Glasgow's heavy
industry, there were inner city areas with population densities of well
over 900 people per acre.[5]

In fact I was wrong to think that generations of city fathers had
simply ignored the horrors of industrialisation. Faced with huge
increases in population and desperate squalor they rapidly abandoned
the idea that market forces would alleviate the city's social problems.

They decided that the city itself must intervene to make the city habitable for all citizens, including that majority who were not noticeable beneficiaries of the industrial boom. An observer wrote that a resident of the city

. . . may live in a municipal house; he may walk along the municipal street, or ride in the municipal tramcar and watch the municipal dust cart collecting the refuse which is used to fertilise the municipal farm. Then he may turn to the municipal market, buy a steak from an animal killed in the municipal slaughter-house, and cook it by the municipal gas stove. For his recreation he can choose amongst municipal libraries, municipal art galleries and municipal music in municipal parks. Should he fall ill, he can ring up his doctor on the municipal telephone, or he may be taken to the municipal hospital in the municipal ambulance by a municipal policeman. Should he be so unfortunate as to get on fire, he will be put out by a municipal fireman, using municipal water; after which he will, perhaps, forgo the enjoyment of a municipal bath, though he may find it necessary to get a new suit in the municipal old-clothes market.[6]

This comment can be read, according to the reader's choice, as either a commendation or a condemnation of local authority activity. The point is that it was made over 85 years ago, long before municipal enterprise could be praised or decried as socialism. For some readers it will indicate how many fields of municipal endeavour have long since been lost to unelected bodies. For others it will suggest that political battles about the relative merits of public or private enterprise in the cities are not really relevant to the actual needs of the city dweller.

The Victorians were faced not with a golden age but with a nightmare, an urban explosion on the same scale as that which has faced the cities of Latin America or Africa in the last 40 years.

When Queen Victoria came to the throne in 1837 there were only five places in England and Wales outside London with a population of 100,000 or more. In 1800 there had been none. By 1891 there were 23. Between 1841 and 1891 the population of London increased from 1,873,676 (11.75 per cent of the total population of England and Wales) to 4,232,118 (14.52 per cent of the total population). In 1841 only 17.27 per cent of the population lived in London and cities of 100,000 inhabitants or

more: by 1891 the proportion had risen to 31.82 per cent. In
Scotland, Glasgow exerted an even greater pull than London did
in England. It contained 5.1 per cent of the population of
Scotland in 1801, 8.6 per cent in 1831, 11.5 per cent in 1851 and
19.4 per cent in 1891.[7]

Historians have tended to see the general attitude of Victorian
legislators to the problems of the majority of city dwellers as a kind of
callous indifference combined with the pursuit of profit. More recent
observers of the period are inclined to congratulate them in retrospect
on the relative success they managed to achieve in circumstances of
pell-mell urban growth on a scale which no previous human society
had ever seen.[8] For example, the historian of the attempts to provide
London with a safe water supply in the face of periodic typhoid and
cholera epidemics, writes of the pioneers: 'To them, at least, whatever
may have been their doubts about the explicitly political implications
of municipalisation, interventionism and collectivism, the salvation
of the city was nothing less than a binding moral duty.'[9]

Somehow phrases like 'binding moral duty' which would have
been perfectly understood in the city politics of Manchester,
Birmingham, Glasgow or Leeds in the nineteenth-century 'golden
age', in the devastating crisis of uncontrollable city growth, have
dropped out of the language of urban politics when we are faced with
an equally unprecedented problem at the end of the twentieth
century, that of industrial collapse.

What alarms me most about the patterns of urban growth and
decline at the end of the century is not that they exist, but that we have
not, for the most part, been prepared to accept a binding moral duty
to smooth the impact of this process. All the great nineteenth-century
sages deplored what was happening to the cities then, just a handful
predicted the pattern of change. Industrialisation was a fact that
people had to accommodate themselves to as best they could. De-
industrialisation is an equally obvious fact, outside the scope of
praise or blame, which we ought to have the will, if not the binding
moral duty, to manage with immensely greater resources than the
Victorians had at their command.

There is no worse error than a problem wrongly stated. Our failure
to grasp the nature of the crisis of our cities exemplifies this, and leads
us to seek solutions by adopting policies that are expensive,
sometimes profitable, but all too often irrelevant. We all acquire in
childhood a mental picture of the city as a finite thing, enclosed by
that most powerful of images, a wall. Beyond it lies the country,

devoted to food production, and, beyond that, the wilderness. This symbolic vision of the city was accurate in medieval times. It was still understandable when the steam engine concentrated power and populations and created an urban proletariat. But it has been woefully inadequate as a key to understanding urban civilisation throughout the twentieth century when the city exploded into the city region, even though political, administrative and fiscal boundaries have seldom recognised this fact.

Even professional planners have always been concerned to fight the battle before last. The geographer Peter Hall comments on this historical irony:

In the 1920s and 1930s, they waged battle against the evils of 19th century industrialism, just as the market was showing a way out to the suburbs. The war – at least in some countries – belatedly made the idea of planning respectable, at any rate to the establishment of the day; and that, in turn, allowed not merely the production of plans, but also the development of administrative machinery that might permit their realisation. But the immediate result was perverse. In the 1950s and 1960s, the age that now comes to be seen as the golden age of dynamic capitalism, planners sought to impose a steady-state view of the city derived from the stagnant 1930s. In the 1970s, as growth flagged, they produced plans for metropolitan expansion. Only belatedly, during the 1980s, are they coming to terms with a new reality of metropolitan decline.[10]

Yet in our personal lives the new realities are obvious. Most British, European or American families now live in suburbs, and an increasing number live not in the suburbs of the nineteenth-century cities, but in those of small towns in the hinterland.[11] The dispersal of energy sources and of communications have not only made the Victorian city obsolete, but they are also pushing into history the giant factory, the huge assembly line, and even the enormous office full of typists and filing clerks.

A century ago, elected to the chair of the infant London County Council, Lord Rosebery declared that 'I am always haunted by the awfulness of London.' It seemed to him, 'a tumour, an elephantiasis, sucking into its gorged system half the life and the blood and bone of rural districts'. His contemporaries of every political persuasion would all have rejoiced that, by the end of the twentieth century, the problem of the cities had been reduced to manageable proportions, not so much by political action but by economic and demographic change. They would simply wonder why it had taken us so long, and why we had failed to cope with what seemed to them a vital issue – that of urban land valuation, which in some cities still stands in the way of rational policies.

For the very language we use about the 'decline' of the cities is misleading, and certainly inaccurate historically. Our cities expanded at a terrifying rate in one short period of urban civilisation. Thus, at the absolute heyday of their alleged prosperity (when heavy industry was loaded with orders, when Britain was the workshop of the world and when its ports were full of ships and ship-building), cities like Glasgow, Liverpool, Manchester, Newcastle upon Tyne or London were notorious for their poverty, their overcrowded slums, their terrifying juvenile mortality, crime, prostitution, disease and destitution, as well as for the existence of an untamed, savage urban underclass.

Every single prophet, propagandist or social critic in the Victorian period was united in condemnation of the exploding British cities of their day. They might be sanitary reformers like James Kay, John Simon or Edwin Chadwick, novelists like Dickens, George Eliot, Disraeli or Elizabeth Gaskell, or moralists like Carlyle, Engels, Arnold, Ruskin or Henry George; the list is endless. Or they might simply be practical people of every political persuasion, or none. The historian William Fishman, himself the grandchild of immigrants living in inner city poverty, recently selected for microscopic examination one particular year, 1888, in the life of the inner East End of London. A series of unfashionable heroes emerge from his narrative: Dr Thomas Barnardo, the Reverend Samuel Barnett, General William Booth, Ben Tillett and Annie Besant. They were familiar with every single issue that arises in the late twentieth-century inner city, from sweated labour and virulent racial prejudice to the sexual exploitation of children or drug dependency.[12]

When the 'inner city', as such, is discussed as a social problem, the description is not used as a geographical expression at all. The phrase does not describe derelict or run-down buildings. It is used as a euphemism for the urban poor. The 'inner city' is an idea rather than a place. We insist on using the words as a kind of shorthand for poor people, often indeed for those immigrant minorities for whom poor city districts are, as they have been throughout history, a 'zone of transition', a point of entry into the urban economy.

But the fact that we use the words 'inner city' to describe the landscape of the poor, anywhere, presents two difficulties. One is that it is adopted in the press and among politicians to describe any area, anywhere, that is perceived as a 'problem'. I have seen it employed, for example, to describe Kirkby on Merseyside, or Southall, outside inner London, in ways which make topography meaningless. Peter Hall concluded in vain, summarising the *eleven* published volumes of research in his *Final Report* of the Social Science Research Council's Inner City Working Party, first, that most inner city residents are not poor and, secondly, that most poor people live outside the inner city.[13]

My further difficulty arises from this, and has also to do with the inflated language used by politicians and administrators. The abolition of poverty is a worthy aim, pursued by some people throughout history. It is not actually on the agenda of policy makers in the cities. But the yardstick by which to judge the success or failure of inner city policies can only be the extent to which they enhance the opportunities – whether in housing, work or education – of poor city dwellers. Since they are seen as the 'problem', only an improvement of their situation can be seen as a solution.

In these terms there are four criteria by which we can assess both accidental trends and deliberate policies in inner city areas:

1. Do they help or hinder low-income families in joining the thinning-out process, taken totally for granted by the more affluent all through this century?
2. Do they assist or obstruct the expansion of dweller-control in housing, once more taken for granted by those with a freedom of choice, but only slowly penetrating the inner city?
3. Do they encourage 'the greening of the city', seizing the opportunity of urban depopulation to create the universally desired environment that people leave the city to find?
4. Do they provide a fine-grain city with small-scale specialised industry generating every level of work, and the kind of informal education that promotes these work opportunities?

CHAPTER 2

AFTER THE URBAN EXPLOSION

Faced with the appalling problems of the instant industrial city, the Victorians attempted to cope with the apparently endless difficulties that surrounded them, either with public health measures, legislation or philanthropy, local or national initiatives. There were a handful of thinkers, however, who attempted to see their own situation in broader and longer historical terms. They form a tradition of regionalist and decentralist approaches to the problem of the industrial city that the urban geographer Peter Hall sums up as the *anarchist* inheritance. He says that 'For me, however unrealistic or incoherent, the anarchist fathers had a magnificent vision of the possibilities of urban civilisation, which deserves to be remembered and celebrated.'[1] It is indeed odd that the most realistic interpreters of the future of cities should be found in this particular minority of Victorian thinkers. Steve Platt comments that 'From Patrick Geddes and the Regional Planning Association of America to Ebenezer Howard and the UK Town and Country Planning Association, there has been a vibrant anarchist tradition, going back to early libertarian idealists like Kropotkin and Reclus, Owen and Morris.'[2]

But if we need guidelines to the future of cities they are to be found in this particular group of prophets. William Morris, designer and socialist, had a subtle and relevant view of industrialism. Looking back from the twenty-first century in his *News from Nowhere*, he wrote:

This is how we stand. England was once a country of clearings amongst woods and wastes, with a few towns interspersed, which were fortresses for the feudal army, markets for the folk, gathering places for the craftsmen. It then became a country of huge and foul gambling dens, surrounded by an ill-kept, poverty-stricken farm, pillaged by the masters of the workshops.

It is now a garden, where nothing is wasted and nothing is spoilt, with the necessary dwellings, sheds and workshops scattered up and down the country, all neat and trim and pretty. For indeed, we should be too much ashamed of ourselves if we allowed the making of goods, even on a large scale, to carry with it the appearance even, of desolation and misery.[3]

The deliberate simplicity of Morris's language cannot conceal his accurate summary of British history, nor the fact that we all share his aspirations for our future.

The second of these visionaries was Patrick Geddes, the astonishing Scottish biologist who urged us to see the city in its regional setting and who argued that planning is 'the development of a local life . . . capable of improvement and development in its own way and upon its own foundations, not something which can be done from above, on general principles easily laid down, which can be learned in one place and imitated in another'. Geddes approached urban management from a completely decentralist standpoint. In 1912 he declared that 'For fulfilment there must be a resorption of government into the body of the community. How? By cultivating the habit of direct action instead of waiting upon representative agencies', and at the end of the First World War, when electoral slogans were about building a Britain fit for heroes to live in, he cried:

The central government says, 'Homes for heroes? We are prepared to supply all these things from Whitehall; at any rate to supervise them; to our minds much the same thing.' But are they? Can they? With what results, what achievements? At present we have the provinces all bowing to Westminster, which (after ample expenses have been deducted) is returned to some of them in the alluring form of a grant. But why not use this money themselves in the first place? Why not keep your money, your artists and your scientists, your orators and your planners – and do up your city yourselves?[4]

Geddes saw the city as the prime *educator* of its citizens, and his rhetoric challenges all our assumptions about the city, its scope and its management. The third of these Victorian confronters of accepted wisdom about the cities was Peter Kropotkin, geographer and anarchist, who foresaw with remarkable accuracy that the industrial supremacy of Britain and the old industrial nations was inevitably to be shortlived, and that we should plan accordingly. Ninety years ago he argued for decentralisation, both on a national and an international scale. He wrote that

> The scattering of industries over the country – so as to bring the factory amidst the fields, to make agriculture derive all those profits which it always finds in being combined with industry and to produce a combination of industrial with agricultural work – is surely the next step to be taken ... This step is imposed by the necessity for each healthy man and woman to spend a part of their lives in manual work in the free air; and it will be rendered the more necessary when the great social movements, which have now become unavoidable, come to disturb the present international trade, and compel each nation to revert to her own resources for her own maintenance.[5]

Kropotkin's conclusion that 'the scattering of industries amidst the civilised nations will be necessarily followed by a further scattering of factories over the territories of each nation' was a uniquely accurate forecast, and Lewis Mumford comments that

> Kropotkin realized that the new means of rapid transit and communication, coupled with the transmission of electric power in a network, rather than a one-dimensional line, made the small community on a par in essential technical facilities with the overcongested city. By the same token, rural occupations once isolated and below the economic and cultural level of the city could have the advantages of scientific intelligence, group organisation and animated activities, originally a big city monopoly; and with this the hard and fast division between urban and rural, between industrial worker and farm worker, would break down too. Kropotkin understood these implications before the invention of the motor car, the radio, the motion picture, the television system, and the world-wide telephone – though each of these inventions further confirmed his penetrating diagnosis by equalizing advantages between the central metropolis and the once peripheral and utterly dependent small communities. With the small unit as a basis, he saw the opportunity for a more responsible and responsive local life, with greater scope for the human agents who were neglected and frustrated by mass organisations.[6]

Mumford himself was writing, it is interesting to reflect, long before computerisation added its own emphasis to this account of the technical aids to twentieth-century decentralisation.

But there was yet another Victorian sage, Ebenezer Howard – inventor, shorthand-writer and father of the garden city idea – who was also completely outside the accepted professional and political world. He declared in 1904 that 'while the age in which we live is the age of the great closely-compacted, overcrowded city, there are already signs, for those who can read them, of a coming change so great and so momentous that the twentieth century will be known as the period of the great exodus'.[7] The trend of census returns, both on the place of residence and nature of employment, throughout this century has supported the forecasts of all these neglected prophets of actual changes, at an increasing pace during the last two decades.

Ninety years ago Howard borrowed £50 from his brother-in-law to ensure the publication of his book *Tomorrow: A Peaceful Path to Real Reform*, later continually reprinted and translated as *Garden Cities of Tomorrow*.[8] It was a clever amalgamation of existing ideas and trends, culminating in his vision of the social city, the many-centred city region as the logical outcome of easy communications and the dispersal of motive power, and combining the advantages of both rural and urban living.

Howard's apparently naïve diagram of the Three Magnets (Town, Country and Town-Country) exercising their different pulls on an iron bar labelled 'The People: Where will they go?' has become the most famous expression of the ideology of town and country planning throughout the world. He forecast what he called a 'Social City', a network of garden cities or town clusters as the future pattern of settlement. I have borrowed from his most famous disciple, Frederic Osborn, the following summary of the main components of Howard's vision:

1. *Planned dispersal*: The organised outward migration of industries and people to towns of sufficient size to provide the services, variety of occupations, and level of culture needed by a balanced cross-section of modern society.
2. *Limit of town size*: The growth of towns to be limited, in order that their inhabitants may live near work, shops, social centres and each other, and also near open country.
3. *Amenities*: The internal texture of towns to be open enough to allow for houses with private gardens, adequate space for schools and other functional purposes, and pleasant parks and parkways.
4. *Town and country relationships*: The town area to be defined, and

a large area around it to be reserved permanently for agriculture;
thus enabling the farm people to be assured of a nearby market
and cultural centre, and the town people to have the benefit of a
country situation.

5. *Planning control*: Pre-planning of the whole town framework,
   including the road-scheme, and functional zoning; the fixing of
   maximum densities; the control of building as to quality and
   design, but allowing for individual variety; skilful planting and
   landscape gardening design.

6. *Neighbourhoods*: The town to be divided into wards, each to some
   extent a developmental and social entity.

7. *Unified landownership*: The whole site, including the agricultural
   zone, to be under quasi-public or trust ownership; making
   possible planning control through leasehold covenants, and
   securing the social element in land value for the community.

8. *Municipal and co-operative enterprise*: Progressive experimenta-
   tion in new forms of social enterprise in certain fields, without
   abandoning a general individual freedom in industry and trade.[9]

Any reader inclined to disdain this list of requirements should
pause for a moment and reflect on the degree to which it coincides
with her or his own personal or family priorities in deciding to move
house. Howard himself was convinced that working models were
more convincing than theoretical arguments, and heroically initiated
two garden cities of his own – Letchworth before the First World War
and Welwyn after it. By modern standards they were absurdly
undercapitalised, but they are flourishing today and Letchworth has
the distinction of being the one town in Britain where the profits
made by the rise in site values are, by Act of Parliament, spent for the
benefit of its citizens.[10]

Howard's ventures eventually led, with the support of all political
parties, to the postwar programme of building over 30 New Towns,
culminating in the new city of Milton Keynes. There were also, of
course, a large number of new out-county housing estates both before
and after the Second World War – from Becontree to Thamesmead,
or from Chelmsley Wood to Kirkby – which are often described as
'New Towns', but which were very far from the concept. For, from
the beginning, they lacked the planned development of industry and
social facilities, and turned poor city dwellers into poor commuters,
obliged to spend on fares the income that might have been spent on
food.

To a third generation, the New Towns have by now become old

towns. They are part of the landscape, and we can recognise that
behind their success or failure are factors that neither Howard nor his
advocates could have envisaged. How could they know that Stevenage
would be a boom town today just because of vast aerospace and
defence contracts, that Skelmersdale would be condemned to hopeless
deprivation for lack of them, or that remote decisions about the
future of the international steel industry would write off Corby? Or,
for that matter, that Nissan would come to the rescue of Washington,
County Durham?

I have seen too much of both New Towns and fringe housing
estates to dare to generalise about local and national policies. I well
remember the woman in Cantril Farm (now renamed Stockbridge
Village) who, as an ex-Liverpudlian, said 'I just wish I was back in the
Dingle', but I equally well recall another woman, originally from the
same place, who said, when I knocked on her door at The Brow,
Runcorn New Town, 'It's Utopia. I never dreamt I would live in such
a lovely place.' In Milton Keynes I talked to a couple, as remote as
could be from the new high-flyers of the computer industry alleged to
populate that place, who simply said that they had lived for 44 years
in Townmead Road, Fulham, and had never expected to achieve a
bathroom of their own.

Taken together, the New Towns have provided a remarkable
return on the initial government expenditure, a return that has never
been compared with the huge sums which have been poured into the
inner cities since the Second World War. It is seldom asked whether
that cash was wisely spent or not. Indeed, by the 1970s the word was
getting around in the academic chat-shows, and thence to the
politicians, that the very success of the New Towns had in some way
been won at the expense of the inner cities. In vain the advocates of
the New Towns stressed that they had absorbed only a small
proportion of the natural outward movement from the cities (8 per
cent in the case of London), and that the greater proportion of the
jobs they generated were new. (Less than one-sixteenth were transferred in the case of Milton Keynes.) Development corporation assets
have for years been sold off in the private market, and they have
proved a very profitable investment indeed.[11] This, of course, has
been the absolute opposite of Ebenezer Howard's hopes, rejected by
history, that the 'betterment value' of land (the difference between its
worth as rural land and its price in the heart of the city) belongs to the
people who created it. Obviously, in the absence of any legislation to
ensure this (with the unique exception of Letchworth), the longer any
New Town corporation, or the Commission for the New Towns

as the residuary body, can cling on to the assets, the greater their market value.

David Hall of the Town and Country Planning Association remarked years ago that a direct comparison would demonstrate that 'a lot of the money that has been spent in inner cities in the postwar period has been mis-spent'. He said in 1977 that

> I did hear a figure the other day that £12,000 million of public money had been spent in Glasgow since the war. That sounds absolutely astronomical and to my mind it is astronomical. I'll bet my bottom dollar that if that figure were converted to some per capita expression of dwellings or jobs or road length provided in Glasgow, compared with the same service provision in East Kilbride, it will have been proved to have been a vastly cheaper investment in East Kilbride.[12]

He was aware that a direct comparison was not possible, nor even desirable, but in ordinary financial terms the New Towns have been a very profitable monetary investment. The irony is that no sooner had the whole New Town episode been thrust into history, than the British experience became important once again.[13] In the first place, the mechanism of the development corporation, thrust upon usually unwilling local authorities in the 1950s in rural areas, has become the chosen vehicle for inner city renewal in the 1980s, imposed by central government upon usually unwilling urban local authorities.

In the second place, the new 'sunbelt' industries of the M4 growth corridor through Berkshire, Hampshire, Wiltshire and Avon are almost unique in the range of vacant jobs available today.[14] People travel great distances for interviews, are accepted, consider lodging in the area just for the sake of the work, and finally retire defeated, just because there is no way in which they could either rent or buy a house.

> Employers have tried bringing workers from Birmingham and south Wales into the Thames Valley on Sunday nights, putting them up in local digs, and shipping them home again after work on Fridays. Such schemes, born of desperation, seldom survive long, as the transported workers tire of the weekly commute, and are always looking for jobs nearer home.[15]

If ever there was a case for inventing a New Town corporation to rush up rental housing just to cater for people desperately anxious to move from areas of large-scale unemployment, and yearning to fill the vacancies with their particular skills, it is there. But there is a third reason why we need an attempt at planned rural expansion instead of the current disappearance of any provision for outward migration from the cities by people who could not possibly buy their way into house ownership.

Ebenezer Howard advocated dispersal precisely in order to make possible the humane redevelopment of the inner city. He thought, 90 years ago, that once the city had been 'demagnetized', once large numbers of people had been convinced that 'they can better their condition in every way by migrating elsewhere', the bubble of the monopoly value of inner city land would burst. 'But let us notice', he wrote in his chapter about the future of London, 'how each person in migrating from London, while making the burden of ground rents less heavy for those who remain, will (unless there is some change in the law) make the burden of rates on the ratepayers of London yet heavier.' He thought that the change to lower urban densities would be effected 'not at the expense of the ratepayers, but almost entirely at the expense of the landlord class'.[16]

It has not happened that way, precisely because of our continued failure to cope with the problem of urban land values. But the relative success of the New Towns (Howard's unexpected grandchildren), led to an understandable demand that the same formula should be applied to the inner cities. The original development corporations of the 1940s were modelled on the pattern of public enterprise set up by Lord Reith with the BBC in the 1920s, or by Herbert Morrison with the London Passenger Transport Board of the 1930s.

In applying the experience to the 1980s, it is regrettable that organisational thinking had not become more sophisticated. In Glasgow the Eastern Area Renewal Project, undertaken by the Scottish Development Agency, lacked the powers of a development corporation and, consequently, was obliged to gain the active support of local authorities in aiming to act in the interests of local residents. In London the Docklands Development Corporation (LDDC) was imposed over the heads both of local authorities and local community groups, after decades of publicly financed discussion of the future of the area. The result has been an unprecedented building boom, exciting to watch, but irrelevant and often harmful to local housing needs and local employment. This is not in dispute. The LDDC admits it and wants to do better in subsequent phases. We have, however, moved a very long way from the vision of the social city that was self-evident to Ebenezer Howard.

CHAPTER 3

DEATH OF THE FINE-GRAIN CITY

The traditional city had a fine grain. Apart from its large public buildings it had developed as a series of small building sites. In Britain the ancient medieval core was developed on plots with what was known as a 'burgage' width of up to 10 metres which tended to dictate the scale of rebuilding and renewal for centuries afterwards.[1] In the much more recent cities of the United States, despite their grid-iron layout, development – whether industrial, commercial or residential – was based upon small 'lots'.[2]

This fine-grain development, despite its complexity, was transparent to the user, by comparison with the sheer opacity of the modern city. There used to be a sense of location which every citizen would acquire quite unconsciously, usually as children. It was developed to a virtuoso extent by people whose work took them to one city after another. For example, old-style commercial travellers in the days when they travelled by train, or people in the world of show business doing the rounds of the theatres, antedated the work of the Chicago school of urban geographers in knowing unerringly the structure of any city. Their ankles told them the way to the riverside, their noses told them they were entering the heavy-industry sector, they instinctively empathised with the great nineteenth-century railway engineers in locating the central station.

Similarly, a city fancier knew without seeing that there must be a lorry-driver's snack bar around the next corner, as accurately as any predecessor centuries earlier would locate a coaching inn. A poor traveller would know where he could find cheap lodgings and the prospect of casual work. An itinerant salesman would know that a shop on that particular site would not pick up enough trade to be safe for credit. A lecher knew, without any red lights, where the red-light district was. Drinkers knew where to find their particular kind of bar. Criminologists could take one look at a place and predict the pattern of offences. Wholesalers and hucksters, junk men and junkies, model airplane enthusiasts and people selling leotards to dancing academies all developed a city sense which is a guide to the specialised functions for which cities originally arose.

The functions and functioning of the city were apparent from its built form. But in the redeveloped city of the last four decades our intuitions have been destroyed. Policies of comprehensive redevelopment – originally instigated by local authorities after wartime bombing, continued when, running out of bomb-sites, they created their own, and then taken over by private developers practising the art of site-accumulation – have eliminated the understandable city. This loss of the sense of place was well described by a Scottish writer, James Finlayson, in a pamphlet with the challenging title *Urban Devastation: The Planning of Incarceration*. One of the identifiers of a sense of location, he observed, was a hierarchy of roads and pavements which often exists in new developments

. . . but does not read as a hierarchy because the functions (themselves hierarchical) which it should describe are no longer visually expressed in the urban fabric. As the logic of the road and street patterns of the old cities collapses, people now need signposted directions to the community centre, to the shops, to the library, provided of course that such 'amenities' have been thought of. In old towns and cities, the environment told people where they were, the buildings 'spoke' to them and 'gave them directions'.[3]

He was right of course. The buildings of the rebuilt city do not talk any more, at least not in a language that makes sense to the citizen. Even the signposts are addressed to the out-of-town motorist, not to the pedestrian citizens who are still the majority of any city's population. There always was, of course, a quieter, gentler and more responsive approach to city redevelopment, stemming from the notions of 'conservative surgery' preached and practised by Patrick Geddes, with the intention of combining the conservation of the whole with the renewal of the parts, cherishing rather than eliminating the *genius loci*.[4] It is also gradually dawning on us that comprehensive redevelopment – with the years of dereliction, of demolition and of subsequent building operations – means, in fact, that after a generation or two, the *whole* environment becomes obsolete simultaneously, so that total destruction and replacement have to happen all over again.

Birmingham is a salutory example. The city grew at an incredible rate in the nineteenth century. The visitor could 'expect to find a street of houses in the autumn where he saw his horse at grass in the spring'.[5] Before the Second World War, the city engineer, Sir Herbert Manzoni, was preparing a long-planned inner-ring road to relieve congestion. The war and the postwar mood gave him the opportunity for wholesale redevelopment to accommodate motor traffic, relegating the pedestrian to a series of bewildering and universally hated underpasses between traffic intersections and multi-level 'integrated' shopping centres. Neither citizens nor strangers can find their way around the city if they are on foot. Traffic in Birmingham, as everywhere else, expands to fit the space made available to it. Now Sir Herbert Manzoni was not an ignorant technocrat spiralling up the local authority promotion circuit. He was a cultivated and dedicated public servant devoted to his city and using the best wisdom of the period to solve its traffic problems. (In retrospect, we could cynically conclude that more fortunate cities had an engineer who was lazy, close to retirement or addicted to golf, as traffic would then have been managed through one-way-systems, park-and-ride provision or neglect, and the physical fabric of the city would have remained intact.)

The most interesting thing about the man who reshaped Birmingham was that he did not personally believe in the viability of the private motor car. I was present myself at a lecture he gave in the 1950s when he declared frankly that

> The present-day motor-car has developed from the horse-drawn carriage; there is every evidence of this development in its form and size and it is probably the most wasteful and uneconomic contrivance which has yet appeared among our personal possessions. The average passenger load of motor-cars in our streets is certainly less than two persons and in terms of transportable load some 400 cubic feet of vehicle weighing over 1 ton is used to convey 4 cubic feet of humanity weighing about 2 hundredweight, the ratios being about 10 to 1 in weight and 100 to 1 in bulk. The economic implication of this situation is ridiculous and I cannot believe it to be permanent.[6]

The Bull Ring Centre in the middle of Birmingham was opened in 1963 after extensive demolition in which the one preserved landmark from the past was St Martin's Church. Traders from the ancient market were rehoused below traffic level, together with an open space named Manzoni Gardens, and surrounded by traffic on three sides. Subsequent new shopping centres, The Pavilions and The Pallasades, were developed on the fringe of the area. By the 1980s the Inner Ring Road, which had destroyed so much of central Birmingham, was seen as a noose, separating the city from its heart. And the Bull Ring itself was, after less than a quarter of a century, seen as a symbol of 'the unfortunate image of Birmingham created in the 1960s – big, brash, overscaled, and lacking in humanity'.[7]

In 1988, therefore, a vast new proposal was submitted by the London and Edinburgh Trust for outline planning permission to redevelop the Bull Ring at a cost of £250 million. A local group, the Association for Urban Quality, issued a critical report to the city councillors which seems, to an ordinary outside observer of the city, to have the stamp of common sense, learning from past errors rather than magnifying them. For the proposal was for a huge structure of incredible size encompassing the whole area, dwarfing and linking the existing shopping centres. It is reported that the architect compared the proposed building to 'a huge aircraft carrier settled on the streetscape of the city'. Negotiations with the market traders led to an agreement to rehouse them in a new space by St Martin's Church, but the one other open space would disappear entirely. The critics say that 'Manzoni Gardens, it must be admitted, is not a good public space. It is poorly and unimaginatively laid out . . . Yet while it remains, it is capable of being turned into a better space. Once it is built over, it is lost forever. It *could* be built over, as long as it is replaced by a better space elsewhere.' But the heart of their objection was precisely that the proposal ignored everything we have learned about the death of the fine-grain city:

Essentially it is *too big*. In the traditional city, street blocks reduce in size the nearer they are to the centre. There are good reasons for this. In a city centre the mixture of uses and buildings gets more complex, and they are all competing for street frontage. The *smaller* the blocks are, the more street frontage there is. This relationship produces a lively city centre – busy streets, varied activity, varied buildings.[8]

I can guarantee that this diagnosis corresponds with the actual experience of every reader of this book. What city would you find most enjoyable and liveable in, and why? Meanwhile the city council appointed a firm of consultants to prepare a scheme for 'humanising Birmingham city centre', and it was reported that 'Large areas would be pedestrianised, subways would be eliminated and the motorway-style inner ring road would be turned into a tree-lined urban boulevard.'[9]

Quick as a flash, the architects for the Bull Ring development responded with an entirely revised scheme (with a value quoted as £400 million) for an entirely new development based on a revival of classical principles of urban design. 'What is more, the new plan offers the city a major new piazza centred on St Martin's Church that, with a little imagination, almost recalls St Peter's in Rome . . . This means that the Bull Ring returns to the city as a public space.'[10]

It must be bewildering to the citizens to see one giant proposal instantly replaced by another with an entirely different character, all in the course of a year, especially as the objectors to the first scheme have, I assume, used up their energy and resources in opposing it, only to be presented by another with an entirely different character which, if it resembles anything, is like Haussmann's redevelopment of Paris. Visitors and residents alike look for the real life of the city in the network of streets and squares left behind by redevelopment, just as in Brasilia they seek out what they regard as the local expression of urban life in the very shanty towns on the fringe where the workers lived, since there was no place for *them* in the new city.

The coarse-grain texture of the redeveloped, financially profitable city slaps you in the face in almost every British town from pavement to skyline, and dressing up large-scale new development in neo-classical detailing does not change the result. It has also changed irretrievably the economic pattern of the city. All those small-scale business enterprises, which provided the incredible range of skills, trades and occupations which were the most important reason why people congregated in cities in the first place, inevitably disappear. For the high rents of new buildings cannot be sustained by the turnover of small businesses, depending on low overheads and on the specialist value of skill, which were originally located there just because they were in the middle of big centres of population.

In ordinary consumer terms this implies no umbrella repairers, account-book rulers, sewing-machine renovators, picture-frame makers, pastry cooks or ballet-shoe makers. No chiropodists, voluntary organisations or small publishers. Only large-scale, highly capitalised, large-turnover and big-profit entrepreneurs need apply. It affects homelessness too. The gradual disappearance of cheap rental accommodation, boarding houses, common lodging houses and even 'reception' beds for the night means that there is nowhere for the poor and homeless to lay their heads. This, of course, is why

there is a growing 'problem' of homeless single people sleeping rough in London or New York today. In some cities there are still cheap, squalid and run-down properties, and consequently somewhere for people to sleep whatever their level of poverty. In the redeveloped city there are none.

But possibly the worst result of the economic rationalisation of the inner city is the way it has destroyed the fine grain of the city economy. Every city once provided a huge range of goods and services in innumerable small workshops, factories and warehouses. Birmingham was famous for a dozen areas specialising in labour-intensive manufactures. The jewellers' quarter survives in a truncated way, the gunsmiths' quarter has been reduced to a couple of streets, other particular, local specialised industries have just disappeared. Sheffield was famous for its 'little masters' in the cutlery trade. Slowly, with the concentration of ownership and the increase in industrial scale, central and local government, politicians and economists all ignored small enterprise in the cities, and often simply swept it aside in the process of redevelopment. The postwar decline of the small workshop sector was less the result of ordinary market forces, as the success of unexpected survivors has shown, than of a sinister combination of planning policies and of land speculation. In the large-scale redevelopment of the cities, small industry was seen as a squalid nuisance, as 'non-conforming users' in substandard premises. Officers of central and local government, trained to think in terms of big-scale industry, simply failed to notice the amount of employment provided in the fine grain of the multiplicity of small businesses dependent on cheap premises and low overheads, and giving both jobs and purchasing power to city dwellers living nearby.[11]

Glasgow's economic fate was dependent on heavy industry, despite the warning signs of its whole experience of the twentieth century, and Andrew Gibb noted 'the failure of the service sector to compensate by expansion for job losses in the manufacturing sector'. He went on to record from that city a by-product of postwar redevelopment everywhere: 'Perhaps more serious in its consequences was the death of hundreds of small enterprises whose low level of capital and low overheads, in brick backyard or railway viaduct premises destroyed by demolition, denied them the possibility of relocation.'[12] Before the Tolmers Village area in the London Borough of Camden was demolished and rebuilt, a survey conducted by local residents found that it contained 105 small businesses employing up to 1,000 people.[13] Readers need only to speculate on the capital

investment involved in 'creating' a thousand jobs to see the effect of this on the local economy.

Until the 1970s train travellers from the south-east of London, in the last lap of their journey between London Bridge Station and the other termini, would look down on a dense network of workshops, warehouses and small factories in the food trades, light engineering, printing and finishing processes. If they were sensitive to the thousands of jobs involved they would have watched with alarm the closing of one after another of these firms. For in the property boom of the 1960s the sites occupied by this myriad of employers became more valuable than the turnover of the humble industries which they accommodated. They were either bought up and closed, or acquired as going concerns soon to be eliminated by the process known as asset-stripping. Instead of that fine grain of individual sites, today's traveller sees a continuous wall of office buildings, providing employment but *not* for local skilled, semi-skilled or unskilled manual workers.[14] It is, however, precisely the loss of *their* jobs, not the increase in office jobs, that constitutes the inner city employment problem. We have slowly discovered the importance of the small-business sector, partly from the unpalatable discovery that large-scale industrial employment is never going to return to the cities, and partly from the fact that small business is virtually the only generator of new industrial jobs.

By the end of the 1980s everyone acknowledges the errors of the 1960s. The arbiters of the city environment invariably say that we should have known better. But it is visible in central Birmingham that the will and the imagination are lacking, and in London the elimination of small industry, on sites that are alleged to be far too valuable to contain it, continues. *Outside* the area of the London Docklands Development Corporation, an engineering firm with 10 employees, built up over 17 years, was told by its landlord that its annual rent would be raised from £3,200 to £21,000.[15] This landlord was no property speculator. It was a London borough which felt it had no choice, since if it failed to raise the rent it would attract the wrath of the auditor as well as financial sanctions from the government. An employer in a neighbouring borough actually said to me, thinking about his overheads and his turnover, 'My enemy isn't in South-East Asia, it's the District Valuer.'

CHAPTER 4

TRAPPED IN THE CITY

People started leaving the city well before the beginning of the century. As the poor moved in, the affluent moved out, aided by the expansion of regular and reliable public transport. Slowly it became possible for a wider spectrum of city dwellers to move out to the suburbs, encouraged by the building of new estates on the urban fringe by both private builders and local authorities. There was once a time in the interwar period when just a few pence weekly separated the rent of a council house and the mortgage repayments on a speculative builder's suburban house.[1] The suburban sprawl of the interwar years was universally deplored by those with a greater freedom of choice, who stigmatised it as jerry-built and shoddy – opinions which are amusing in the light of the prices such houses fetch in the market 50 or 60 years after they were built.

As families moved up from the poverty line their demands were for more space, gardens and leafy surroundings, and these yearnings have been faithfully reflected throughout the twentieth century, just as Ebenezer Howard predicted, by outward movements of population from the cities. Trace the history of innumerable families in Britain and you will find one generation moving to the city to escape rural poverty, another generation establishing itself in the economic life of city workers, and the next moving out again to the suburbs or beyond. Today the whole urban transition is often accomplished in a lifetime: the young drawn to the city for its glamour and opportunities, and then leaving for more space to rear a family. The freedom of choice that this implies is simply a matter of personal income.

In most family life histories, inner city living has been a temporary phenomenon. All the world's cities have had generations of comers and goers. It was true during the alarming growth of British cities in the nineteenth century, just as it is true of the incredible expansion of population in the cities of Latin America and Africa in the second

half of the twentieth century. Displaced peasants have been obliged
to throng to the cities in search of a livelihood and subsequently have
moved out to the periphery or beyond in search of a better life, more
space and more opportunities for their children.

They and not their circumstances have always been blamed for the
evils associated with urban poverty. In the last century, when Social
Darwinism was an acceptable philosophy, observers used to blame
the problems of the mushrooming cities on the riff-raff of the
population that was emigrating from depressed rural areas. They
suggested that the countryside – whether British, Irish, Galician or
Calabrian – was exporting its thriftless, footloose elements to the
town. At the very same time, observers of what was seen as the crisis
of rural life were lamenting that the able, enterprising, stable, bright
and adventurous members of the village population were the ones
who emigrated, leaving behind those who lacked these qualities or the
opportunities.

A century later, when the cities were losing population, the same
wounding stereotypes were brought into play in reverse. In Britain
the government-sponsored New Towns were blamed for stealing the
most skilled people and the best jobs from the cities. Paradoxically, in
the 1970s, when I had the opportunity to visit most of the New
Towns, teachers and social workers would take me aside and explain
confidentially in the shining new schools that 'we have a terrible lot of
problem families with very little motivation and ambition'. All these
subjective impressions are relative, of course, and are often based on
nothing more tangible than our well-known English snobbery. Ex-
urbanite commuters living in old towns and villages beyond green
belts would not be seen dead in anything so plebeian as a New Town,
precisely because the planned New and Expanded Towns provided
rented housing for people who, at the time, could not conceivably
hope to buy. Sir Frederick Gibberd, the architect-planner of Harlow,
told me with some pride that he was the only New Town designer who
lived in the town of his creation.

The exodus from the cities continues. Immigration or the inward
flow of the young and mobile do not affect the statistical trend. But
the opportunities for low-income people to join this outward
movement have steadily diminished, even though the evaporation of
traditional urban industrial jobs has increased the motivation for
mobility. The establishment of green belts, with all-party support,
has produced a situation characterised by Peter Hall years ago as 'a
civilised form of apartheid'. The rich can buy their way into the green
belt, the commuting middle classes can leapfrog over it into new

settlements or old country towns and villages beyond it. But the poor are trapped for lack of mortgage-worthiness. This is made amply clear in Martin Elson's magisterial study of the impact of green belt policy.[2] Professor Lewis Keeble comments on what he calls the unacceptable face of this sacrosanct aspect of environmental ideology: 'How lovely to own a house in an area – town edge, village or green belt – where competition has been removed. Most of the good people who appear at public enquiries to object to development do not, I think, realise that they are supporting gross and unprincipled greed.'[3]

The programme of New and Expanding Towns had similarly been supported by all parties until it was wound down by a Labour government in the 1970s. Yet, at the very time of the switch in policy, one of the government-commissioned Inner Area Studies, made it perfectly clear that, contrary to the conventional wisdom, excessive population pressure in London 'had been insufficiently relieved by decentralisation, either planned or unplanned'.[4] Ten years later, an examination of employment problems in London stressed that 'the very selectivity of decentralization, in which genuine opportunities for movement were available only to those who had access to owner-occupation or who possessed the skills then required in the New and Expanded Towns, has done much to produce this situation'.[5] Maurice Ash, as chairman of the Town and Country Planning Association, declared that the combination of efforts to shore up the inner cities amounted, in practice, to nothing less than a conspiracy to *contain* the disadvantaged, 'a conspiracy', he said, 'because it suits the policies of our centralized state to keep the cities as prisons for the poor. It suits both those who want to manipulate the poor for reasons of power, and those who want to keep them from the preserves of the rich.'[6]

If this is seen as an extreme view, it is shared in an unexpected quarter. Every summer a caravan of wanderers in old buses and caravans converge in the vicinity of Stonehenge and infuriate residents, the police and newspaper readers. They are known as the Hippy Convoy and are seen as a squalid nuisance. They seldom have an opportunity to explain their point of view, but when they do they support the opinion of Maurice Ash:

Several members interviewed contrasted the convoy way of life explicitly with living in the cities, and described it as a consciously chosen alternative. They feared that the current harassment and impounding of vehicles is likely to leave them with no choice but to go back to the cities. They talked about a difference in quality of life between being unemployed in the city and unemployed in the community of the convoy. They talked about their right to choose the convoy way of life and not to be forced to live in the city. In choosing *mobile* accommodation, the convoyers are effectively exploiting the *only* remaining loophole (thanks to the traditional rights of bona fide gypsies and holiday caravanners) available to people without cash, mortgage credit-worthiness or access to New Town rented accommodation who nevertheless are determined to escape the city – a loophole which, as we can see, is currently being mercilessly tightened.[7]

There was a time when desperate solutions like that of wandering around rural England in old buses would have seemed ludicrous. Strange though it may seem to the modern reader, there was a period in the first 40 years of this century when, as Anthony King explains in his history of the bungalow,

A combination of cheap land and transport, prefabricated materials, and the owner's labour and skills, had given back to the ordinary people of the land, the opportunity denied to them for over two hundred years, an opportunity which, at the time, was still available to almost half of the world's non-industrial populations: the freedom for a man to build his own house. It was a freedom that was to be very short-lived.[8]

He is referring to those areas known to planners as the 'plotlands', places where, as a result of the agricultural depression and the collapse of rural land prices, sites were sold for as little as £3 a plot for city dwellers to build their holiday shanty, weekend home, bungalow or would-be smallholding. These sites were to be found all over south Essex, in the Thames Valley, the Weald of Kent and Sussex, and notoriously at Jaywick Sands. The makeshift landscape that resulted was, like the 'suburban sprawl' or the 'bungaloid growth', deplored by all right-thinking (i.e., well-housed) people and has been outlawed by postwar planning legislation.

Such housing was not, however, despised by its inhabitants, who were often poor families from the East End of London, and wherever a policy of benign neglect has been adopted by planning authorities the properties have been endlessly improved by their owners and are gratefully lived in today by their grandchildren. Dennis Hardy and I had the opportunity to interview dozens of the original settlers, typified by Mrs Granger who borrowed a pound for the deposit on her plot in 1932 and said to me: 'We never had a mortgage for any of the houses where we have lived. I feel so sorry for young couples these days, who don't get the kind of chance we had.'[9]

Since the 1970s a whole series of proposals and experiments have sought to bring together the experience of the original garden cities, the New Towns and the plotlanders. They include the Do-it-Yourself New Town[10] the Third Garden City[11] the Greentown Group,[12] and the Town and Country Planning Association's Lightmoor project.[13] They have all had a single aim: to enable people with low incomes who want to leave the city to do so. By the 1980s this group has been joined by another category with an urgent claim to housing: the adult children of rural families who have no chance of housing themselves because of the escalation of rural house prices resulting from the exodus of the affluent from the cities. For the enormous irony is that these people now have to migrate to the nearest available town to rent bed-sitting rooms, not because they want to but because they have no other option.

There are, of course, a dozen proposals by consortia of builders for private enterprise new towns and new villages. They are excellent in themselves but can only be useful for low-income city dwellers if they include low-rent housing or provision for modest self-build schemes. This is why, after 90 years of garden city propaganda, the Town and Country Planning Association has still to argue the same case as the most rational, most economical and least environmentally damaging response to needs which remain unmet. David Hall urged in 1988 that, instead of building more homes on the fringe of existing rural communities, at least 12 garden cities – in the tradition of Welwyn and Letchworth, with a balance of homes for *all* incomes, space for jobs and a good environment – should be built. They would, he claimed, take pressure off the green belt and embattled towns and villages, provide affordable homes for the less well-off in the south-east and for people trapped in high-density, inner city blocks of flats, guarantee badly needed public open space in the cities, and lay down both 'go' and 'no-go' areas for the south-east, where they would

. . . be part of a proper strategy, linked to policies that divert growth to the disadvantaged regions of the north . . . The communities of the south-east are suffering from *ad hoc* house-building. The solution to housing need is not to cram people into the inner cities, but to rediscover the idea of garden cities. The careful location of garden cities of different sizes would be the best way of minimising the impact on people's 'backyards', while meeting most of the need. All this means planning, and it means selective intervention by government to achieve valuable objectives that will benefit everyone.[14]

This is in fact a sensible case, convincingly expressed. But for political reasons which have nothing to do with its merits, it is unlikely to be put into effect, at least until we have learned the consequences of an absence of policy. We can draw a general conclusion that (with exceptions) New Towns were imposed by Labour governments upon unwilling Conservative local authorities, while Urban Development Corporations, modelled on the New Town Development Corporations, tend (with exceptions) to be imposed by a Conservative government upon unwilling Labour local authorities.

But if David Hall's solution is to be dismissed as wishful thinking, it is worth considering the fantasy offered by Ferdinand Mount, an anti-planning free marketeer who was stung by the inappropriate comments made by the Prince of Wales on a visit to Bengali residents of Spitalfields in East London. Mr Mount first imagined a benevolent, 'if rather tactless and insensitive dictator', and then asked what such a person would do about poverty and unemployment. His own suggested answer began:

> Well he might start by abolishing all planning restrictions and also declare, with the generous agreement of the Royal family, that all royal parks and estates were henceforth public building land open to all who lacked a roof over their heads. In no time, chalets would mushroom over the grounds of Highgrove as the Bengalis took Prince Charles's offer of help literally. Other ill-housed immigrants would soon do the same in the policies of Gatcombe and Nether Lypiatt. Their children would grow up strong and healthy in the Cotswold air. The rural economy of Gloucestershire would be immensely invigorated, restoring to the county some of its former medieval glories in the textile trades. It should be said, *en passant*, that in order to make housing genuinely cheap, our dictator would probably suspend the Parker Morris housing standards . . .

He went on to forecast that

> The price of building land would plummet, the rate of house-

building would soar . . . Some of the houses might be a little
tacky, others would have a rustic charm; the total effect would
certainly be far more attractive than Broadwater Farm or the
Liverpool Piggeries. Businesses, large and small, would multiply,
much of it in the South no doubt, but the boom would certainly
spread to the Dales and the Peak District. Jobs would multiply,
and employers in southern England would at last be able to fill
all their vacancies, since workers in the North would now be able
to buy or lease their chalets for a song or build them with their
own hands on a pleasant and convenient site.[15]

This engaging dream is an idealised version of the 'plotland'
history mentioned above, and it directly addresses the situation of
those who are trapped in the city. But it hangs upon a fantasy from
the Middle Ages – a benevolent dictator and royal benevolence. In
real life we have to rely on the long, tedious and time-consuming
process of patiently setting out a rational proposal and building up a
lobby to support it. Planning is out of fashion, and these are not
propitious times for such an endeavour. But planning in this context
means, not fussing about building standards and elevational controls
but a determination to manipulate site valuation so as to give the
urban poor the same opportunities and the same freedom of
movement that are taken totally for granted by the affluent.

Stephen Holley – who was for years the general manager of
Washington New Town in County Durham, and consequently
watched with a growing exasperation the unaccountable shifts in
central government policy – expressed his feelings in verse as follows:

> Isn't it a pity about the Inner City?
> People leave who shouldn't ought
> And that affects the rate support.
> If only those who stayed behind
> Had left instead, no one would mind.[16]

CHAPTER 5

BRINGING IN THE TASK FORCE

A long time ago I accepted an invitation to take part in a conference about the problems of the inner cities. It was convened on the assumption that if only you could bring together all the participants in one room, some kind of harmony would result. We listened to the views of the then government and the Opposition, local politicians and the representatives of every kind of interest group. Harmony did not result, but at the end of the day Professor Ray Pahl tried to sum up the differences of approach.[1] He found that the six mutually diverse interest groups were:

1. Those who believed in the 'technological fix'. They were the Whitehall and local authority executives who saw themselves as the pre-eminent providers of services and facilities, with a heavy emphasis on professional and managerial skills.
2. The political radicals who believed that the professionals were engaged in a conspiracy against the public for their own aggrandisement. They further believed that nothing could be solved without changing the whole system.
3. The populist, anarchist, a-political movements who also believed in the conspiracy of the professionals, but who declared that people could and should do something now.
4. Those who shared the mistrust of the professionals, but saw answers in the arts, crafts and community work, declaring that small is beautiful.
5. The pragmatic realists who knew in their practical hearts that in the end piecemeal amelioration would be called in to do the job.
6. The one-off fixers whose approach was: bring in the consultants, sort out priorities, put a figure and a time-limit to the job and then throw in the task force.

Professor Pahl did us all a service in stressing the incompatibility of these approaches. It clears the air if we admit that we do not agree on methods or objectives in tackling inner city issues. We are also singularly lacking the means to assess or evaluate the impact of any of these approaches. Governments have a weakness for the military analogies of the 'task force' approach since they express the resolve that *something* will be done. All my life they have been committed to the abolition of the slums. Now they are committed to grander aims: the abolition of poverty, or of unemployment, or of crime, ignorance or ill-health. In the event, these impossible aims recede as a new government initiates another programme and another task force. The introduction to a recent volume on urban history made the terse little comment that 'having demolished slums which stood for a century, we constructed homes which lasted a decade'. Unfair? Untrue? Most people in most British cities will readily think of examples. The authors declared that 'damp, boredom, vandalism and garbage undermined the urban vision'.[2]

The urban visionary in Newcastle upon Tyne was a famous council leader, T. Dan Smith. In his memoirs he describes how 'I hired a Rapide aircraft to make flying visits to see candidates for our new appointment of a Planning Officer . . . Local government had moved from a parish pump era into the big business league . . .'[3] He found the 'forceful' character he was seeking in the form of Wilfred Burns, who in his book *New Towns for Old* explained that 'the dwellers in a slum area are almost a separate race of people, with different values, aspirations and ways of living . . . Most people who live in slums have no views on their environment at all.'[4]

Furthermore, 'when we are dealing with people who have no initiative or civic pride, the task, surely, is to break up such groupings even though the people seem to be satisfied with their miserable environment and seem to enjoy an extrovert social life in their own locality'.[5] The historian of the postwar redevelopment of British cities, Alison Ravetz, notes that

> . . . a major feature of the New Brasilia that Burns created, to the satisfaction of both Smith and his Conservative successors, was a motorway ring, part of the national trunk road system, which formed a wall inside which were impressive precincts for council offices, commerce and education. Those who were about to lose their homes or livelihoods to make way for the new polytechnic were issued with a free booklet explaining the importance of higher education for the future prosperity and leisure of the town.[6]

Anyone who has watched the modern evolution of Newcastle upon Tyne will appreciate the depths of irony in this comment. The city's planning officer went on to become Sir Wilfred and the central government's chief planner. I rejoiced to learn, at yet another meeting, that his own appreciation of local residents' perception of their environment had changed completely. He said that

People have many different perspectives on their environment and on community life but only now are we beginning to see these articulated. It is not all that many years ago since people trusted local or central government to analyse their problems and prescribe the solutions. Those were the days when people accepted that new and exciting developments were bound to be better and when change seemed to be welcomed. We then moved into a period when unique prescriptive solutions gave way to the presentation of alternatives so that the public could express views before final decisions were taken. Today we face a different situation. Community groups, voluntary organisations of many kinds, and indeed individuals, now demand a say in the definition of problems and a role in determining and then implementing solutions. Even in the professional field that we normally think of as part of the establishment there are various movements concerned with reinterpreting or changing the professionals' role. Self-help groups of many kinds have sprung up, sometimes around a professional, or at least, advised or guided by a professional. It is quite clear that a number of people believe that the traditional professionals are not able adequately to communicate with people in a way that will help them solve their problems or make their wishes known to those who take the decisions.[7]

This carefully worded admission that city management would never be the same again is very important in view of our long history of governmental policies of bringing in the task force. Ever since the 1920s we have had attempts by various departments of central government to address the problems of declining industries and declining cities. The then Board of Trade addressed itself to encouraging industry into what were successively known as 'depressed' areas, 'distressed' areas and then more euphemistically as 'special' areas, a policy pursued until quite recently through industrial development certificates.

After the war, the cities themselves embarked on 'clean-sweep' policies of urban redevelopment, known to their critics as 'raze and rise'. By the late 1960s the disillusionment, that had been swept away as backward-looking sentimentalism, became too obvious to be ignored. Conservation Areas were defined by the Civic Amenities Act of 1967, General Improvement Areas emerged in the Housing Act of 1969, Housing Action Areas and Housing Priority Areas followed. Community Development Projects had also appeared: central government setting up local teams independent of, and usually critical of, local authorities. They also became critical of the ultimate holders of economic power in British cities, whose far-away decisions could profoundly affect the citizens in ways totally beyond their control or that of their local authorities. The Community Development Projects (CDPs) became an embarrassment and were ended in 1976.[8]

The growing need to be seen to be 'doing something about the cities' was complicated by rivalries between government departments. Since the war, the Department of Industry, heir to the Board of Trade and its discovery of regional problems, had pursued regional policies of industrial dispersal recommended in the wartime Barlow Report and implicit in the New Towns programme. The speech delivered in September 1976 by the Secretary of State for the Environment, Peter Shore, suggesting that regional gains had been won at the expense of the cities (a notion that is historically and statistically unsustainable), signalled a reversal of policy. In the screeching of brakes, the government-sponsored Location of Offices Bureau had to reverse overnight from advising firms to move out of cities to encouraging them to move in. At the same time, the Inner Area Studies – commissioned by an earlier minister, Peter Walker, to report on inner city districts of Liverpool, Birmingham and London – were deeply critical of the 'raze and rise' policies pursued since the war and of the design and management of local authority housing.

The Home Office, too, became involved in inner city policy by way of issues relating to race and immigration. Section 11 of the Local Government Act of 1966 had provided for grants to local authorities for special services to Commonwealth immigrants, a step bitterly criticised by ethnic minority groups for its failure to meet their needs.[9] The original unspoken intention of the CDPs had been an attempt 'to end dependence of deprived groups on local bureaucracies'.[10] From 1974 onwards, the Home Office sponsored Comprehensive Community Programmes, as that department sought to establish some kind of overview. Years later, Lord Scarman felt obliged to report that there was 'a lack of an effective coordinated approach to tackling

inner city problems. Looking at the examples of Brixton and
Merseyside, conflicting policies and priorities – as between central
and local government or between the different layers of local
government – appear to have been a frequent source of confu-
sion . . .'[11] American investigators found that in the United States
'the greater the number and severity of riots in a city or state, the
greater the subsequent local expansion' of federal government
activity there,[12] and in Britain, while there is no direct link between
deprivation and inner city riots, there is a connection between these
events and urban policy, and 'in responding to the 1981, and
especially the 1985 disorders, the central state has looked to improved
police methods and strength (for example, the possible introduction
of plastic bullets) as well as allocating increased urban aid to the
affected cities'.[13]

Behind the scenes in central government, whichever party was in
control, there were intense rivalries between departments. 'A feature
of urban policy in the early 1970s was the struggle between the Home
Office and the Department of the Environment. A decade and a half
later we can observe the struggle between the Department of the
Environment and the Department of Employment (with the Treasury
and the Department of Industry watching closely).'[14] But beyond
these private Whitehall wars has been the ideological colour-
blindness pursued as a matter of policy by both Labour and
Conservative governments and their local equivalents. Gideon Ben-
Tovim of Liverpool sums up this failure of policy with the observation, backed by a mountain of research, that

> A large body of national evidence points to the worsening socio-
> economic position of black people. Many sources have docu-
> mented the disproportionate growth of black unemployment;
> the failure of the black community to make inroads into white
> collar and professional layers of the labour market; the
> difficulties placed in the way of black businesses (e.g. with
> grants, banks, planning permission); the particularly vulnerable
> position of black youth who suffer chronically high rates of
> unemployment and, when involved in government schemes, are
> consistently allocated poorer training and job opportunities
> than their white counterparts. At the local level in Liverpool, for
> example, there has been no change over a long period in the
> broad occupational position of the black population in terms of
> employment by central and local government agencies. The
> reluctance of both central and local government to adopt ethnic

monitoring makes it difficult to quantify precisely the position, but the evidence is that Liverpool City Council still has a less than 1% black proportion of the workforce as a whole.[15]

Local informed critics may have pointed to the failure of central government to meet the issues allegedly involved in coping with urban crises, but since 1981 there has been a bewildering series of new initiatives.

Over a five-year period Urban Development Corporations, Enterprise Zones, Task Forces (Merseyside), Urban Development Grant, City Action Teams, and Task Forces (Employment) have come into being. This proliferation of semi-autonomous and/or centrally accountable institutions and the parallel dilution in the role and function of local authority partnership and programme authorities represents a major shift in the interest and power structure within inner cities policy.[16]

Liverpool, in particular, has suffered from the imposition of every kind of 'bring in the task force' rhetoric for many decades, whatever the flag flying from local or national government, whatever the political colour. As Lord Gifford was conducting an inquiry into the fate of Liverpool 8, seven years after the riots of 1981, a caustic account of government policy reported how 'Civil servants spread thin over six different ministries were given different labels (development corporations, task forces, city action teams) and managers were seconded from private industry. In addition, there was to be safe investment for big business in the form of schemes, gleaming with a coat of pseudo-benefaction.'[17] Years earlier, the Secretary of State for the Environment had taken businessmen on a local tour. Yvonne Roberts sought the results:

Seven years on, the Leeds Building Society has no presence in Liverpool 8. ICI has no involvement in Toxteth. The Prudential has 'nothing specifically in Liverpool'. The Midland Bank has, in conjunction with the DTI, set up a loan scheme not in Toxteth but in the Albert Dock for small businesses: net investment, £200,000 – the price of a London house. In short, Liverpool 8 has no building society, loan scheme or independently funded project. The efforts of the task force have been miniscule. A major refurbishment of housing, conducted through a building society, has yet to employ local labour on a large scale. The

building of the International Garden festival (now bogged down
in bankruptcies) and the Albert Dock, the yuppie Taj Mahal of
the north, required enormous investment by taxpayers and a
very small commitment from private enterprise. Neither project
had any impact at all on Liverpool 8.[18]

Apart from the irresistible attraction of phrases like 'task force'
among those who needed to be seen to be doing something, there are
several points to be noted in the hubbub of government-inspired
policies of special funding for new initiatives in the cities.
   The first is their *ad hoc*, temporary nature. They can be switched off
in the same casual way in which they are switched on. There is no
public evaluation since the brief is so vague and all-inclusive.
Secondly, there is no public accountability, contrasting sharply with
the public scrutiny that central government conducts into the
spending of local government. A third significant point is that the
endless succession of acronyms, initials and central offices ensure
that local groups of citizens have either to develop or to hire the
particular expertise to cope with them, or to go without. They seldom
know which particular government fund or EEC fund can be drawn
upon for their specific initiatives. Finally, while the 'voluntary' or
non-statutory sector has become more and more involved in special
projects funded by central government, its officers have continually
to trim their objectives to make them acceptable:

In 1985/6 there were over four-and-a-half thousand voluntary
projects receiving Urban Programme support involving some
£76m of spending. The pace and extent of this involvement has
had a number of impacts. It has brought about the increased
bureaucratisation of the non-statutory sector and forced many
organisations into an organisational culture and style quite
unsuited to their functions . . .[19]

On the other hand, local authorities have been increasingly
excluded, even though the Department of the Environment White
Paper of 1977, *Policy for the Inner Cities*, declared that 'local
authorities are the natural agencies to tackle inner city problems.
They have wide powers and substantial resources. They are
democratically accountable bodies . . . their local judgement of needs
and solutions will be essential . . .'[20] Councils themselves have a
lamentable record in the cities, but ordinary observation records a
falling away in ordinary council services which are not connected

with special programmes, simultaneously with the emergence of special programmes. When Housing Action Areas and General Improvement Areas were first mooted, public meetings of residents were held to ascertain *their* priorities. Invariably, what the citizens asked for were simple services, which were the original reason for the existence of the authorities: better street cleaning and refuse collection, improved street lighting and maintenance generally – items which one special programme after another was not empowered to provide.

The Archbishop of Canterbury's Commission on Urban Priority Areas made this amply clear:

> . . . the shift in the balance of policy to secure the greater involvement of the private sector in particular, has gone side-by-side with major reductions in central financial assistance to UPA local authorities despite resources for the Urban Programme nearly doubling in cash terms between 1979/80 and 1983/84. Local authorities in many UPAs have lost far more in Rate Support Grant than they have gained under the Urban Programme. There has been an overall decline in central government financial support. Although the Urban Programme – the icing – has grown in real terms, the cake – the 'bending' of main policies and programmes – has either shrunk or disappeared altogether. There is one exception: the only main central government expenditure programme to have shown a significant growth in the inner cities in real terms since 1979 is that on the police.[21]

The point is spelt out in detail by the Town and Country Planning Association, reporting that 'Manchester City Council gained in real terms, an extra £9 million via the urban programme between 1980/81 and 1984/85 while losing some £100 million in Rate Support Grant settlements within the same period', while in London in the period 1979/80 to 1983/84 'Inner London gained £261 million in Urban Programme funding while losing £865 million in Rate Support Grant and a sizeable proportion of the £791 million of housing subsidy lost to London (1980/81 prices).'[22]

It is hard to escape the conclusion that the 'bring in the task force' ideology has been used by both Labour and Conservative governments to conceal this reduction of ordinary public services. There are plenty of cities where the local authority in its various guises is the biggest employer, especially the biggest employer of low-skilled or unskilled labour. Municipal services tend to be labour-intensive and a policy of cutting down on them is bound, in the absence of alternative employment, to produce personal and family misery in one more household. It can, therefore, demonstrably result in an actual increase in costs to the public purse. The Town and Country Planning Association, once more, expresses the point well.

The distressing irony of this situation is such that not only does high unemployment mean a waste of human resources (and millions of individual personal tragedies) but it is extremely costly in cash terms for which there is little or no economic return, certainly none which benefits the inner city areas. Edinburgh University's Department of Social Administration has estimated that in 1985 the direct Exchequer costs of unemployment amounted to nearly £20 billion. This amounts to £6,300 per registered unemployed person. If local authority costs are included the total arises to about £6,800 per person.[23]

There could be no more persuasive illustration of the way in which disposing of one superfluous refuse collector or street cleaner in the name of efficiency just adds to the public budget, while the streets remain dirty.

CHAPTER 6

TALES OF TWO CITIES

One of the effects of the Second World War was to remind the whole population of the condition of the inner cities. The conscription of both young men and young women, and the evacuation of city children, in particular, revealed both to city dwellers and to their fellow citizens elsewhere that when the London docks were at the height of their prosperity, when Liverpool was at the hub of world shipping and when Glasgow was exporting industrial goods to every continent, the people employed in this Indian summer of productivity for the workshop of the world were living in conditions of dreadful overcrowding.

Both London and Glasgow suffered a devastating loss of industrial employment in the postwar decades. Public policy encouraged large numbers of residents to move out. Some wanted to and were happily able to. I have talked to dozens of former Dockland residents in Basildon New Town in Essex, and to dozens more Glaswegians who moved to East Kilbride and Cumbernauld, who had all made a successful transition, as well as to less happy families who failed to remake their lives in the fringe estates of both cities.

Policies of wholesale demolition obliged many inner city dwellers who did not want to move, to be transplanted or to be rehoused within the city itself without the jobs that had sustained their households. This left 83 per cent of residents in Limehouse as tenants of Tower Hamlets Council in London; and in Glasgow, a city which always does things in a grandiose way, the council tore down acres of its old housing years before it could hope to rebuild, 'thereby wreaking social havoc and wasting resources on a colossal scale'. The authors of this comment also remark that 'What this community has passed through is in some ways rather like a major war.'[1]

It did indeed leave a population pyramid, in statistical terms, rather like that of a war-ravaged nation. No one with any knowledge

of the grotesque overcrowding of the East End of Glasgow will regret
that its population declined from 150,000 in 1948 to 40,000 in 1986.
Inner London underwent a comparable change. Apart from the
immense fall in population following wartime bombing and
subsequent outward movement, 'between 1966 and 1971, while the
population for Greater London as a whole fell by 5 per cent, in the
five Dockland boroughs as a whole (Tower Hamlets, Southwark,
Newham, Greenwich and Lewisham) the rate of decline was 10 per
cent, rising to 18 per cent in Tower Hamlets'.[2] By the 1970s the
population of the Dockland area itself was about 55,000, a figure
comparable to that of Wapping and Shadwell, a small part of the
total area, in the mid-nineteenth century. In terms of living and
working space, the difficulties had been reduced to manageable
proportions. But the characteristics of both areas remained those of
deprivation. Dennis Hardy's diagnosis of this dismal catalogue in the
East London Dockland area is identical with any social estimate of
Glasgow's East End:

> . . . infant mortality rates, numbers suffering from respiratory
> diseases, hospital admissions, truancy and crime rates, and
> higher education entrants all scored badly for Docklands. On a
> specific issue, that of claimed welfare benefits, the rate in Tower
> Hamlets in 1971 was nearly twice that for Greater London as a
> whole. Throughout the 1970s the downward spiral of economic
> and population decline took with it what remained of the area's
> local services. Public transport facilities were notoriously
> inadequate, with limited and unreliable bus services, dilapidated
> stations, and long and tedious journeys to central London only a
> few miles away. Residents in different parts of Docklands
> complained, with justification, about local medical services –
> with a shortage of doctors, chemists and clinics. There were no
> major shopping centres within the area, a dearth of open spaces
> for recreation and, generally, a poor and depressing environ-
> ment. Docklands was well and truly in decline.[3]

In both areas, measures to cope with all these symptoms of
multiple deprivation seemed to be long overdue. And in both cases
they were seen to be beyond the scope of the instant task force
approach, the mere semblance of remedial activity. They needed a
longer time-span and a far greater commitment of public resources.
We have seen how the development corporation ideology, adopted
for the postwar New Towns and proving profitable, has attracted

people who wanted to cope with inner city desolation. The Town and Country Planning Association has advocated this use since 1966 and continues to press for Urban Development Corporations (UDCs) with a series of specific assumptions, that:

1. UDCs should only be set up within a particular inner city area if the local authority agrees.
2. UDCs should be required to produce a publicly agreed planning and development strategy for their areas which must be related to the planning strategies for the whole of the urban areas in which they are located.
3. UDCs should be obliged by their terms of reference to set up an ongoing consultation process with local people so as to determine their needs and wishes.
4. UDC boards should have a small majority of their members drawn from the local authorities for that area.[4]

These formal, almost formalistic, requirements have not been met by government in decisions to establish UDCs, but nor have the needs which Dennis Hardy described: the decline of ordinary municipal services, of transportation, of health provision, and the running-down of schools in the wake of population decline and, above all, of housing maintenance. As we saw in the last chapter, the availability of some special fund of central government largesse fails to counter-balance the reductions in public spending which fall, almost inevitably, with the hardest impact on declining communities.

The Glasgow Eastern Area Renewal project (GEAR) antedates the adoption of UDCs. It was started in 1976 and was, at the time, the largest urban renewal scheme in Europe, following the switch in central government policy from New Towns to inner city. Work had been about to begin on Stonehouse New Town but this was abandoned, with the subsequent transfer of resources and personnel to GEAR. The project covered a large area of eastern Glasgow, bringing together several agencies of central and local government (some of them peculiar to Scotland, such as the Scottish Development Agency and the Scottish Special Housing Association), as well as the district council and the Strathclyde Regional Council. Its intentions, in the words of the then Secretary of State for Scotland, were to achieve

> ... the comprehensive rehabilitation of a major sector of the City [through] the application of resources to a single large area,

without making any additional call on the ratepayers or reducing the resources available for the redevelopment of the rest of the City. The remit will cover the planning and development of the social, environmental and industrial life of the area . . . The Scottish Development Agency would also contribute by carrying out its own functions of derelict land clearance and environmental improvement by building factories and helping to fill them with employment-creating projects, and by supporting appropriate commercial developments.[5]

The secretary of state had proposed the full planning powers of a development corporation, but refrained from pursuing this aim in deference to the regional and district councils.[6] David Donnison and Alan Middleton conducted, not an evaluation, but an attempt to assess the lessons of GEAR, and they commented that

The fact that the Scottish Development Agency lacked the powers of an Urban Development Corporation and therefore had to gain the support of the local authorities was probably an advantage. The fact that the area chosen for renewal was inhabited by some 40,000 fairly belligerent people who compelled the agency to set up an office in the east end and deal frankly with them was another advantage.[7]

Rather than ask the study team whether GEAR has 'succeeded' or 'failed' they thought it more sensible to see it as a test-bed for various ideas and policies. In fact, in this hastily conceived project there was 'a lack of clear and meaningful objectives'. Instead there was a crab-wise movement, just to satisfy public expectations, with 'no statement of overriding priorities'.[8] They stress the fact that GEAR is simply the biggest of a dozen policies that, ever since the wholesale demolitions of the 1950s and 1960s, have come and gone according to fashions in central government policy and subsidy.

The efforts to bring new sources of employment to the area have not brought any startling successes, but since so many heads of households there are not eligible for employment, good housing is much more important than job-creation. But the existence of the project has made little difference to housing in the area, except as part of Glasgow's wider policies of supporting community-based housing associations and co-operatives. In view of the scale of council ownership of housing there, David Clapham and Keith Kintrea conclude that 'decentralisation in Glasgow will have to go much

further if it is to make any impact on residents' involvement'.[9] If
GEAR has done little to bring prospects of local employment for
local people or to dramatically improve housing, what has it
achieved? Undoubtedly the East End environment has been improved
dramatically and, as Sheila McDonald remarks, 'A city can be
labelled every bit as destructively as a difficult-to-let housing estate,
and Glasgow was so labelled. Shedding that stigma is a slow and
costly process in which the GEAR project plays an important part.'[10]

   I wandered around the area, looking for a few once-familiar
landmarks. Some were there, transformed by the ordinary process of
cleaning, others had been replaced by new, attractive housing. Large
old buildings had been sublet to small enterprises. Like any other
visitor, I was staggered by the greening of Glasgow's East End. David
Donnison in fact believes that the cost of maintaining the new
landscape will be so high that 'much of it may eventually be allowed
to run wild'. This is no disaster, he thinks. City wildscape is valuable.
He suggests that the budget should be turned over to local groups and
that there should be more opportunities for 'self-maintenance' by the
provision of allotments and space for maintaining motor vehicles and
for learning-to-drive teams. In the middle of the area, I came across
the Barrowfield estate, which at first sight seemed to have benefited
little from the investment in GEAR. 'You didn't see it ten years ago',
Bill Nicol of the Barrowfield Community Association expostulated.
Here is an estate of 600 tenement flats, built around an immensely
wide road leading nowhere (part of an abandoned highway scheme),
and which has been stigmatised from the moment it was completed. It
has been the subject of a whole series of official programmes in the
past, and even GEAR's support has wavered. David Clapham refers
mildly to the 'scepticism of many residents who have seen concerned
officials come and go with other initiatives in the past'. Very slowly,
flats have been renovated, the empty ones filled, gardens have
appeared, and Barrowfield Community Business is 'providing
significant economic and social dividends'.

   Around the corner in battered old premises (not like the renovated
carpet factory known as the Doge's Palace, which has become the
Templeton Business Centre), I saw new small firms, in businesses like
flooring and upholstery, tool hire, buying and selling surplus pallets
and 'period surrounds and fabrications', creeping into that huge void
in Glasgow's industries left by the heavy engineering that has gone for
ever. John Pearce, chief executive of Strathclyde Community
Business, says: 'There are Barrowfields now throughout Britain and

it is in communities like this that people have been increasingly asking the question: what can we do to create jobs, to tackle our own problems?'[11]

The Dockland areas of East London have several common problems with the East End of Glasgow. There is the same devastating loss of the major local industries, as the docks closed one by one. There is the same heavy dependence upon local authority housing where standards of maintenance have steadily declined year by year. For years there has been the same decline in ordinary public services and there is the same low expectation of employment among school-leavers. Dennis Hardy, in his study of the area, comments that

As the various docks finally closed their gates at the end of the 1960s, so the planners gradually moved in. A seemingly immortal vision of the East End as a centre for heavy industry focussed around the docks themselves – solid and unchanging – was replaced by a new and disturbing perspective of an inner city in crisis. Existing planning authorities were called into action, and new planning agencies with a Docklands-wide brief were formed. It could be expected that, as public bodies, whatever changes they could bring to the area would be in the 'public interest'. Yet experience has shown that the public interest is an illusory and misleading concept, and general agreement as to how Docklands should be redeveloped is inevitably a goal that is always just beyond reach.[12]

This was not for want of effort. A series of measures by central government was applied to the area, from the Urban Programme of 1969 onwards. In the period from 1970 to 1974, first Peter Walker, as Secretary of State for the Environment, commissioned the first studies of possible redevelopment of the area. Then his successor, Geoffrey Rippon, set up the Docklands Joint Committee to co-ordinate the various planning authorities. The succeeding government introduced the Community Land Act of 1975, which in this particular context would 'end the paradox of high land values in decaying areas' enabling local authorities to buy land at existing use values, but 'it was a measure that promised much but yielded very little, securing only a few acres for Docklands development'.[13] The Inner Urban Areas Act of 1978 established 'inner city partnerships', intended to bring together local and national government agencies for co-ordinated action. It allocated Urban Programme funds for environmental and social programmes and gave the boroughs new powers to encourage local industry.

Meanwhile, the London Docklands Study Team commissioned by Peter Walker had reported on a series of options, explaining that 'No plan can please all, and in selecting a particular plan the community as a whole will be choosing to meet the demands of some and to turn down, in part or completely, the claims of others. The selection of a plan must be part of the general political process in the community . . .'[14] The team set out in detail five particular options. One was 'Waterside', based on a Thames-side park and housing which would add 74,000 people to the population with new river crossings linking the area with office and shopping centres. Another was 'Thames Park', with still more emphasis on new public open space. A third was 'East End Consolidated', reviving traditional patterns of rented housing and developing new local industrial jobs. The fourth was 'Europa', based on private housing and a rapid transit system. Finally, 'City New Town' proposed redevelopment on the pattern of the existing New Towns, with a town centre on the Isle of Dogs and improved transport systems. It was expected that the boroughs and local community groups would favour one or other, or a combination of several. But as Dennis Hardy puts it:

> Instead, 'the general political process in the community' rejected all five – lock, stock and barrel. There was bitter resentment that consultation had not taken place in the formative stages of plan-making, and a justified suspicion that land would be used for City and West End uses which would be of little benefit to many people already living in the area. Four of the five options proposed, to differing degrees, luxury housing, marinas, office development and tourist schemes.[15]

The apparently endless stalemate was resolved by the incoming government of 1979 with its provision for UDCs in the Local Government Planning and Land Act of 1980. This empowered the Secretary of State for the Environment to designate any area of land as an Urban Development Area if he is 'of the opinion that it is expedient in the national interest'. The purpose of a UDC is 'to secure the regeneration of its area' by 'bringing land and buildings into effective use, encouraging the development of existing and new industry and commerce, creating an attractive environment and ensuring that housing and social facilities are available to encourage people to live and work in the area'.[16]

The London Docklands Development Corporation (LDDC) and the Merseyside Development Corporation (which covered an area of Liverpool Docks with very few inhabitants) were set up in 1981. In 1987 the government designated five more UDCs, in Cardiff Bay, the Black Country, Tyne and Wear, Trafford Park and Teesside. Later it proposed a further three in Bristol, Leeds and central Manchester, as well as an expansion of the Black Country UDC. In 1988 there were proposals to extend the area of the Merseyside UDC and to establish one in Sheffield. It is evident that the Docklands experience is considered to be a success. A House of Commons report concluded that 'The UDCs pattern arose from the frustration of the administration at the apparent inability of the local authorities, in many cases after repeated attempts, to achieve the nationally important task of solving the problems of these difficult areas, which the new bodies were expected to take by the scruff of the neck.'[17]

This comment seems to me to be quite near the truth. It presupposes, however, that central government can find solutions to urban industrial decline which are beyond the reach of the councillors. They would readily respond that they have for years been starved of the funding that has been pumped into the LDDC: 'Between the institution of the UDCs and the end of 1986–87, £380 million has been spent by the LDDC (including £315 million grant-in-aid from the DoE and £60 million from land sales).'[18] Nothing in the professional ideologies of local government officers had prepared them for the inevitable departure of traditional sources of employment, and the record of local councils has been as bad as that of the incoming Development Corporation in this respect. Nick Wates and Charles Knevitt provide a scarifying account of the ineptitude of both council and Development Corporation in a detailed history of what happened in Limehouse.[19] But a whole host of local community bodies, from the dockland fringe of the City of London itself, eastwards through Wapping, the Isle of Dogs, Canning Town and the wilderness of the former Beckton Gas Works, have endlessly sought the merest recognition that they have a point of view. It is many years now since Ted Johns, now active in the Association of Island Communities, declared the independence of the Isle of Dogs, as a reminder to the outside world of what was going to happen. All his misgivings about the future have come true. His patch has become a suburb of Hong Kong, 'a massive, gleaming financial centre surrounded by a shanty town'.[20]

At the bottom end of the Isle of Dogs I found Michael Barraclough. He moved there at a time when the area was 'red-lined' by the building societies as a place where no mortgages were to be granted. He was obliged to join with others in a building venture, and ever since has been the co-ordinator for 'community developed housing'. One of his first involvements was with the Shadwell Basin Project, in 1974 when the local children in The Highway threw stones at his car. While angrily chasing them he noticed that first one and then another lorry was tipping its load of demolition rubbish into Shadwell Basin. 'What a waste of a useful space', he thought, and his subsequent approach to the youth workers in that area led to the setting up of the project. Another of his activities has been with half-a-dozen, self-build housing associations in the area. Set up by local residents, frequently the adult children of families rehoused in tower blocks, these associations have relied on a precarious viability which rests on site valuations. These, as assessed by the district valuer, increased uncontrollably from £175,000 an acre in 1985 to £1,600,000 an acre in 1987.[21] It is an enormous tribute to the people involved that any housing at all, at affordable rents, has been provided in the Docklands area, and most of all to those who have striven, through self-build associations and housing co-operatives, to battle against these devastating odds.

For, unlike the New Town development corporations upon which they were modelled, the UDCs have no responsibility for housing. The people displaced by their activities are left to the mercy of the local authorities, carefully deprived of funding by the self-same government which thrust this additional responsibility upon them. You do not have to have the slightest sympathy with the councils concerned, who have mismanaged their housing for years, to feel outraged by the way in which local inhabitants have been brushed aside, like the Indians or the Aborigines in the colonisation of America or Australia. It is an ordinary fact of life that the new luxury housing that affronts them has been bought and kept empty because the anticipated increase in value makes speculation more profitable than occupation.

But just as distressing as the part played by the LDDC in reducing the opportunities for rehousing local people, has been its role in the decline of employment. The accelerating rise in site values made some employers realise that their sites were more lucrative than their turnover.

A joint survey by the Docklands Consultative Committee, Docklands Forum and London Borough of Newham (Sept. 1987) of Newham's Riverside Industrial Belt has shown that

more than 6,000 jobs have been lost in 6 years, and this in an area
where 82% of jobs are in the manufacturing sector. The LDDC
has actively encouraged industrial firms to relocate from areas
such as the Surrey Docks, where one local firm – WBS Transport
– was offered £1.2 million to relocate from Greenland Dock with
a loss of 400 jobs. The firm has subsequently ceased trading. It
was announced in May 1987 that the Peak Freans factory in
Bermondsey would close in the New Year with the loss of 1022
jobs, of which half live locally in Southwark.[22]

The same story can be multiplied all over the Docklands area (like
Tate & Lyle's decision to drop 586 jobs on their Plaistow Wharf site
so as to 'take advantage of the new economic circumstances').[23] The
situation of really small business was described by the House of
Commons all-party Select Committee on Employment which found
that the LDDC had, through its activities, destroyed thousands of
existing blue-collar jobs. It concluded that 'UDCs cannot be regarded
as a success if buildings and land are regenerated but the local
communities are by-passed and do not benefit from regeneration'.[24]
    We can travel on the new Docklands Light Railway and look down
on new building activity which is a tonic for anyone who has seen this
area sinking into decay for the last 30 years. But the nagging thought
remains that neither GEAR in Glasgow nor the LDDC in London
have significantly improved the housing situation or the employment
situation of the actual residents. This apparently simple task has
eluded every official body. In the case of London it was not even on
the agenda. Yet they are at the heart of the real inner city issues for
anyone who takes seriously the endless series of governmental
interventions, and wonders why they have not worked.

CHAPTER 7

VICTIMS OF SUCCESS:
THE AMERICAN WARNING

In the beautifully restored Benedum Theatre in Pittsburgh, where I was a guest of the American Institute of Architects, civic leaders proudly explained that the renovation of that theatre, as well as the building of the Vista International Hotel where we had spent the week debating the remaking of cities, owed much to the federal government's Urban Development Action Grant Programme. Privately I had heard the view expressed from people on both the political right and left that developers had cynically steered the federal funds into projects which would have happened anyway.[1] Publicly I heard just one voice, that of Alan Mallach, a housing advocate from New Jersey, urging more urgent priorities. He told us that

> The concept of a public/private partnership as a relationship between two sectors – government and the private market – is flawed by its exclusion of a third essential actor – the residents of the community affected. Self-congratulatory messages about entrepreneurial successes and the proliferation of shiny down-town office buildings obscure the reality that many people do not benefit from all this success, and many are deeply and permanently harmed.

Mr Mallach was heard in silence.

He had been an expert witness in what became known as the first and second Mount Laurel trials of 1975 and 1983, when the New Jersey Supreme Court first enunciated and then reaffirmed what became known as the Mount Laurel doctrine. This ruled that every municipality *must* 'by its land use regulations, make realistically possible an appropriate variety and choice of housing. It cannot foreclose the opportunity and . . . must affirmatively afford the opportunity . . . for low and moderate income housing.'[2] I was resigned to the expectation that Mr Mallach's dissenting opinion would be completely ignored. For all eyes were focused on the next speaker, the honorary chairman of that conference. But what he said reinforced everything that Alan Mallach had said, and everything I had learned from the experience of urban revitalisation in the United States and Britain. The traffic in downtown Pittsburgh had been halted, security men scrutinised the assembled guests, as the chairman closed the conference with the following words: 'If the money motive for development is the only serious force in urban renewal, then we shall not succeed. There is *less* chance of getting things seriously wrong if sensible and effective ways are found of consulting the existing inhabitants of our cities.'[3]

This was indeed the message I derived from the cities I visited in the United States. I was following in the footsteps of several British government ministers – Kenneth Baker, Norman Fowler and Kenneth Clarke – and some of the same civic leaders who were patient with them (like Mayor Schmoke of Baltimore and Mayor Young of Atlanta) were equally patient with me. They *knew*, after all, the appalling problems they face. I came back from the same lightning visits with a totally different impression.

Mr Baker made everyone laugh by praising the New York public school system. The people I met despaired of it and, in other cities, those who actually understood how the education machine works, whether as teachers or parents, thought that American city schools were run for the benefit of the administrative machine and neither for the pupils nor the hard-pressed staff. They looked back to the 1960s not as a time of romantic illusions, but as a period when, with all those experimental street schools and store-front schools, a handful of people actually had the nerve, and could get the funding, to set up alternatives.

Mr Fowler went to look at 'workfare', the schemes adopted in several cities which aimed to get people off 'welfare' and into work, using various degrees of pressure. On his return, he firmly denied that he wanted to see such programmes introduced in Britain. I think that his denial stems from the discovery that local legislation in, for example, Boston, requires that specified proportions of jobs in public employment or publicly supported contracts are reserved for local residents, or for women, or for members of ethnic minorities. This is not at all a theoretical issue. I have seen sites in the London Docklands where, before anyone knew that they were financial goldmines, trees and vegetation had grown up which were valuable to the inhabitants. Then they became designated for 'landscaping' and everything was bulldozed and new planting was introduced, the whole exercise, whether justified or not, being conducted by an outside contractor with imported labour, contributing nothing to the turnover in the local shops.

Mr Clarke confidently said that the United States is the only country in the world from which we can learn how to cope with inner city issues.[4] Like everyone else, he used the word 'partnership' to describe the conjuncture of public and private funding. He urged British cities to learn from the great 'turn-around' that has happened in Boston, Atlanta, Baltimore and Philadelphia. I have followed the ministerial trail in each of these cities. My overwhelming impression everywhere was that once you are out of the downtown revitalisation belt you move into areas of poverty on a Third World scale, with creeping rehabilitation by people who can afford to buy those romantic colonial houses. Yes, of course it creates new jobs, but these are for cleaners, dishwashers and sweepers, who cannot conceivably pay the enhanced rents. One of Mayor Young's aides in Atlanta drove me around the unofficial city, where a demonstration claimed, at the moment when the nation's architects were meeting in Pittsburgh, that 'It is a disgrace that we have men and women falling in the gaps of the so-called safety net onto the sidewalks of every city in the nation.'[5] At the same time, in the same city, a group of teachers known as Rich's Academy were pursuing an alternative school for 100 drop-outs, a 'school of last resort',[6] while every week-end a group of students were 'swiftly and illegally erecting a hut to house one of the city's estimated 6,000 to 8,000 homeless people . . . suddenly appearing at night in carefully scouted warehouse districts, wooded areas and even vacant lots adjoining residential neighbourhoods, to build huts for the homeless, providing immediate shelter . . .'[7]

I reflected that it might be a sign of the moral health of American cities that everywhere I went I found groups of people actively challenging the official reality of urban renewal by luxury retailers in shopping malls, or by the agents of international computer companies in office blocks. For example, I arrived at one of the world's most famous schools of architecture, that of the Massachusetts Institute of Technology (MIT) at Cambridge, Mass., to talk about the British housing experience. Not a hundred metres from where we sat, Tent City had arisen in Blanche Street, echoing a famous housing struggle in Boston in the 1960s, and its occupants were demanding that three houses there, illegally emptied by MIT, should be made available to the homeless. I learned in the next few days how MIT, founded of course as a poor man's college, had – like its neighbour, Harvard – become a major property owner in Cambridge. Over the years it had enveloped the site once owned by the Simplex Cable and Wire Company and the housing all around. It appointed a firm called Forest City Development to set up a 27-acre project with a luxury hotel, expensive shops and high-rental housing. Pressure from Cambridge City Council and local groups modified these plans to include 300 housing units of which 25 per cent were to be 'affordable'. But MIT could not wait. It ensured that those houses should remain empty for eight years, while waiting for the land assembly, and sanctioned the removal of wiring and plumbing. On 15 November 1987, Cambridge City Council passed a resolution requiring MIT to negotiate their case through an appointed arbitrator. On 19 November, dwellers in Tent City told me that the police chief had visited them with a bag of bread rolls and told them that they could choose among themselves which five should be arrested. At dawn the following day, contractors hired by MIT put the occupants' belongings into four trucks and the police arrested ten people. The Simplex Steering Committee commented that, 'Over the last decade MIT has consistently resisted calls for community involvement in its development plans. All too often, MIT seems to act not as an institution of higher learning concerned with its social responsibilities, but as a private corporation motivated by the drive to profit from its property.'[8] I mention this particular instance simply because I witnessed the arrest of further protesters on the following day, but I suspect that, behind many a story of turning around American cities, there are similar sordid tales of squeezing out the few rights of the poor.

In considering the lessons of the United States, it is important to remember that we are talking about a continent rather than a country. However much the independence of states or cities may have been eroded by the American version of federalism, it would be both inconceivable and impossible for the federal government to abolish local authorities. Both states and cities (often in opposition to each other) have considerable revenue-raising powers in their own right. These may be insufficient, but they are not at the whim of federal control. A further difference from the British situation is that banking and investment are also local. Until a Supreme Court decision of 1985, banks were obliged to be confined to a state. Even today they are regional. It is much easier to promote local investment when credit is not totally awash in the world market, seeking, say, the most currently profitable patch of the Pacific Rim. Much the same applies to American industry which, in contrast to that of Britain, tends to be locally based and to have every reason for embracing a local 'partnership'. With very few exceptions, big British firms have loyalties only to the stock market in the City of London. The fact that one of the few names to rise to the reader's mind is that of Pilkington Brothers of St Helens simply proves this point.

But there are endless reasons why the miracle of Boston cannot be considered as a model for British cities. The first is that access to federal finance is very unevenly distributed. Some cities (like Baltimore and Boston) have been favoured because of geographical, political or financial proximity to Washington, and have been even more favoured because of the distribution of defence and research contracts. Others, with less influence in these fields, have fared worse. The rise in property values has ensured, just as it has in Cambridge, that the poor have been squeezed out. But it is a fact that half of Boston's population and income are directly dependent upon government spending.[9]

One of the visiting ministers, Kenneth Clarke, was thrilled by the revival of Baltimore, which he remembered as 'the ultimate rust-bucket dump ten years ago'.[10] Like him, I was impressed by the spectacular redevelopment of the inner harbour with three new shopping pavilions on what used to be the waterfront. One of these sparkling new developments is devoted entirely to eating. I found this odd considering that the whole culture of affluent America is built around losing weight and, under the eyes of the security guards, I talked to an old man who recalled how, in the bad old days before regeneration, local boys would splash around in rowing boats, picking up fish for the family meal. Grady Clay, the most acute monitor of the American urban scene, reminds us that the reconstruction of downtown Baltimore arose because the civic leaders 'perfected a unique set of linkages with the Federal bureaucracy and the Democratic Party during the crucial 25 years of urban growth and renewal following World War II, and they made the most of it'.[11] He learned from former Mayor Schaefer, later the state governor, that by July 1982, 'the public funds pumped into Baltimore's Charles Center and Inner Harbour redevelopments alone had totalled $199.8 million, of which $137 million or 67 per cent, had come from the federal treasury in grants and subsidies'.[12] What I learned from the present mayor, Kurt Schmoke, is that this was 40 per cent of all the money received from state and federal resources, while the city, from which the poor were steadily being squeezed out, had at least 5,800 empty houses awaiting rehabilitation.

I was not at all surprised to hear Baltimore described as 'the most dependent city in the US',[13] and less than half a mile from the city's downtown miracle I saw the queues forming outside the soup kitchens run by Catholics and Quakers. For, beyond the miracle, Baltimore is the eighth poorest city in the country, with 60 per cent of its households living, in 1988, on an income of less that $15,000 a year. After a few more minutes' walk, I was in the poverty belt to see some of the hard-pressed people struggling to establish the rights of the poor majority to live decently in their own city. Mary Benns of Baltimore Neighbourhoods Inc., Ralph Moore of the St Ambrose Community and Michael Mazepink of the People's Homesteading Group told me of their struggles to get existing housing legislation enforced. A few years ago, the Homesteading Group tried to bring landlord-abandoned houses back into use, not by the sophisticated folk who knew how to exploit urban homesteading, but by those who had been excluded. They took matters into their own hands by occupying their first empty house. Now families who join the scheme undertake to work 480 hours for the group and, in addition, an hour for every hour of group labour provided on their own future home. 'It's not hard work', explained one homesteader. 'You can take a rest, but you feel bad when others are working in front of you.'

I heard similar tales from Carey Shea of the Lower East Side in New York, who told me of the heroic (in terms of the personal bravery needed in the criminal jungle) appropriation of abandoned housing there, where the plumbing and wiring had long since been ripped out and even the staircases had been turned into campfires by junkies:

> People just identify city-owned buildings and take possession. They try to establish themselves as heroes of the surviving neighbourhood (as indeed they really are) to get away from the squatter image. Mayor Koch used to denigrate them and send in the police but now, once they have succeeded, he attends every opening and the city now gives a $15,000 interest-free loan per dwelling.

Edmund Bacon, the architect and planner who struggled for years with the city fathers of Philadelphia, explained to me how hard-won were his attempts to ensure that the centre of a great city should be redeveloped on the scale and with the sense of neighbourliness that the opportunity demanded.[14] The result, in the rebuilt Market Street, is immensely attractive and agreeable. Professor Bacon had won me over. But downtown Philadelphia stays in my mind as the place where I encountered more beggars per 100 metres than in any city I have ever visited. Beneath Gallery 1, the handsome new shopping centre, I took the Patco Line of the Metro and in a quarter of an hour had crossed the Delaware River and emerged, blinking in the sunlight, from the subway at City Hall Station, Camden, New Jersey.

I felt as though I had stepped into a disaster movie. There was an immense, wide street with no cars or people, a vast city hall, an impressive court house and consequently a huddle of lawyers' offices, tall hotels and department stores with their ground-floor windows blocked up. I learned that Camden had once had a ship-building industry, but was now dependent on two employers: RCA, with their defence contracts; and Campbell's, the soup kings.

In the past, Campbell's had brought in parties of Puerto Rican women to pick tomatoes in New Jersey (the Garden State, as it calls itself). But there came a time when it was cheaper to import tomatoes from Florida or California, so the women were instantly out of a job and the growers were without a market. The implications of this ordinary entrepreneurial decision became clearer to me as I walked up to the north side of Camden. Just as in Atlanta, Baltimore or Philadelphia, as the streets got visibly poorer, there were more and more people around. At 644 State Street I finally found Tom Knocke, sweeping the porch after dispensing the umpteenth of many thousands of free meals that come from the Leavenhouse every year. He, like Michael Mazepink in Baltimore, is a former town planner, and learned about city policy from the inside. When I asked him what he would be doing in ten years' time, he replied, 'I'll be here. It's a lifetime commitment.' I was taken aback for several reasons, one of which was that he was evidently quite certain that the problem of places like North Camden is going to get worse rather than better.

There are reasons for his claim. The crash of stock prices in October 1987 led an army of financial advisers to urge investors to put their money in property rather than shares. In New York a television personality called Sonny Block told viewers that Camden, New Jersey was the last place on earth where a housing bargain could still be found. This was music to the ears of the city council, desperate to increase its tax revenue. In a joint enterprise with Rutgers University, it used public money to bring in four busloads of New York investors to size up the Camden property market. The effect was electric. One purchaser bought a house for $39,500 and, without removing the 'For Sale' signs, put it back on the market for $120,000. Another bought a house from the federal government's Department of Housing and Urban Development for $23,310 and put it back on the market a month later for $65,000.

In Camden, New Jersey, smart, city-wise and sophisticated people can buy and sell other people's miserable homes, purely as a market transaction, without the slightest contact with the frequently father-less families who cobble together the cash to pay the rents. The tenants' children have to stay away from school because, being bilingual, they need to translate for their mothers at the welfare office. Later they get involved in the drugs business just because this is the only way open to them to earn real money, as opposed to the meagre earnings of the non-technical staff at RCA or of the fruit-pickers who are now collected by lorry at 4 a.m. to gather labour-intensive products like blueberries and cranberries.

Naturally there is a local response. The Concerned Citizens of North Camden began as a group of squatters who took over abandoned property, subsequently gaining tenure and an improve-ment grant. The North Camden Land Trust has been struggling to acquire the land on which the houses stand, with the aim, as members explained to me, 'to take housing off the speculative market. The trust owns the land while individual families own the buildings. If people move out the trust has the first option. What people put into the house they get back. The aim is simply to keep housing in the hands of local people.' Faced with the fact that traditional sources of finance will not lend (though they are incredibly eager to do so if a New York investor buys the property), it is an endless task for the trustees to gather the capital from a handful of socially aware private investors and from the Delaware Valley County Reinvestment Fund.

The real lessons we can learn from American cities come not from the partnership of government and business but, as Alan Mallach observed, from the residents of the communities involved. A right-wing critic, Stuart Butler, was surprised at the success, against all the odds, of the 'sometimes strange but highly effective' local community organisations and concluded that 'Unlike the millions spent on official projects, which in so many cases seemed to have little if any permanent effect, the community-inspired self-help activities evidently laid the groundwork that first stabilised the area, then became a springboard for recovery.'[15] Everything I learned in the United States supports this view.

CHAPTER 8

STOCK AND FLOW IN THE CITY UNDERCLASS

In his novel *The Dean's December*, Saul Bellow's protagonist, a liberal academic, has a flash of understanding which leads him to realise that all the urban programmes, with their innumerable acronyms, may have provided a livelihood for the people involved in administering them, but had in no way changed the lives or prospects of the poor inner city dwellers of Chicago. These citizens were not needed in the economy, and were in fact just a drag on it, since they were not even consumers of the right kind and quantity of goods. They were simply superfluous people.

His American audience was, in the first place, mildly scandalised. Was not this yet another arrogant sneer directed at the defenceless poor, and all those whose welfare provided a focus of public concern? But the second reaction was one of relief. Someone, admittedly a fictitious character, had raised unmentionable truths and had paved the way to respectability for new, hard, tough attitudes, as the old American left joined the swing towards the new American right. If people are superfluous, there is a limit to the tax income that it is worth expending upon them. It was once again respectable to talk about the 'underclass'.

It is, of course, a very old idea. There has always been an urban underclass. In 1851 Mary Carpenter called them the 'perishing and dangerous classes', Marx dismissed these superfluous people as the 'lumpenproletariat', and in Marxist states they are called social parasites and hooligans. Modern Western Marxists call them the 'reserve army of labour', at a time when the captains of industry are busy demobilising the regular soldiers of this army. A century ago Charles Booth found that 'they degrade whatever they touch, and as individuals are perhaps incapable of improvement; they may be to some extent a necessary evil in every large city'. Fifty years ago a

sanitary inspector, C. R. Martin, linked this self-perpetuating
underclass with immigration as 'the very worst tenants it is possible to
imagine, probably with alien trash thrown in'. It 'consists of people of
varying degrees of viciousness: drunkards, hooligans and loafing
idlers down to the hardened criminals and moral degenerates; men
and women who are monsters of cruelty and soddened with drink,
who prefer to lead lives of filth and crime'. For such degenerates,
many of them Jewish, Negro, Chinese or Irish, the only solution, he
thought, was 'segregation in the form of sanitary imprisonment'.[1]

There was also at that time a revival of interest in the underclass as
it was thought to breed at a greater rate than the general population.
John Macnicol, the historian, explained to me that every effort to
follow the idea of an underclass reproducing itself down the
generations has failed. In the 1970s Sir Keith Joseph claimed that
mothers in social class V were 'producing problem children, the
future unmarried mothers, delinquents, denizens of our borstals,
subnormal educational establishments, prisons, hostels for drifters',
and he declared that 'social workers, teachers and others know only
too well the sort of situation I am referring to'.[2]

Such people, in daily contact with city poverty, are all too aware of
a complex web of disadvantage, but what research has failed to
establish is a hereditary pattern.[3] No statistical evidence supports the
idea of a self-perpetuating underclass. The idea, since it surfaces so
regularly in history, obviously fills a need for the people who believe
in it, so rather than attempt to refute the notion it is perhaps more
useful to introduce the concept from industry and commerce, of
'stock and flow'. This refers to the goods that have to stay on the
shelves until needed and to those which pass through continually.
The same classification is readily applied to the inner city.

One of the functions of inner urban places has always been that of
the 'zone of transition'. Spitalfields in East London, just outside the
ancient city, has for centuries been an area, endlessly stigmatised as
the slum home of an underclass, which forms such a transitional zone
where new arrivals gained their first foothold on the urban economy
and their first induction into city ways. They have left their traces in
the street names, the architecture and the typical local occupations.
Observing the Huguenot silk-weavers, Dickens reported that

> . . . considering that both the worker and the work are
> deteriorated by an obstinate tenure of the present dense and
> unfit site, it seems wonderful that the weavers themselves are not
> as anxious to remove from a noxious and unprofitable

neighbourhood, as their well-wishers can be to effect their removal . . . It is as if the Huguenots had brought their streets along with them, and dropped them down here.

He marvelled that 'they prefer dragging on a miserable existence in their present abodes'.[4] The Huguenots did in fact move on, and so did the Irish who aroused similar comments. They, in turn, were followed by the Jews, a few of whom had been established in the district for centuries, but the vast majority arriving in the great influx that followed the pogroms in the Russian Empire. They, too, were stigmatised as an alien underclass, but as they moved on from the zone of transition, their place has been taken by the Bengalis, working in the same trades, usually in the same buildings.

The evidence from the cities is of a flow. But, increasingly, it is perceived as a stock. And this stock is composed, it is thought, of a new urban underclass. This underclass is believed to consist of people who have never been in gainful employment, who have fallen out of the habit of being useful citizens, and who reproduce themselves at a higher rate than the general population, in each generation. Academics discuss passionately whether or not a 'culture of poverty' exists. Some share Sir Keith Joseph's interpretation of the phrase, others see it as yet another way of stigmatising the poor. For the man who originated the phrase, the anthropologist Oscar Lewis, it meant something quite different. Tired of the way it had been misused, he wrote:

> The culture of poverty is not just a matter of deprivation or disorganisation, a term signifying the absence of something. It is a culture in the traditional anthropological sense in that it provides human beings with a design for living, with a ready-made set of solutions for human problems, and so serves a significant adaptive function. In writing about 'multiproblem' families the scientists . . . often stress their instability, their lack of order, direction and organisation. Yet, as I have observed them, their behaviour seems clearly patterned and reasonably predictable.[5]

People adapt to the situation in which they find themselves. Peter Hall stresses the real significance of Lewis's findings: '. . . by no means all poor people were locked into the culture of poverty; a certain rather special set of conditions had to be met, including a cash economy with high unemployment, lack of any kind of organisation for the poor, lack of extended kinship and a dominant value system that suggested poverty was due to personal inadequacy'. Professor Hall himself, after surveying the immense American literature on the issue of the underclass, concluded that

> A hundred years ago, contemporaries located it among the most desperate of those who had been driven into the slums of the giant city, and who had been least successful there in finding a foothold on the socio-economic ladder. A century later, they find it among the same groups. Meanwhile, countless numbers of the great-grandchildren of that first group have climbed out of the underclass. Doubtless, numberless progeny of the second will prove to do the same. The abiding problem is why, despite all the massive intervening economic and social improvement, the underclass should so steadily recruit new members to replace those lost to it. To that question, research as yet provides no answer.[6]

Where research provides no answer, we are all entitled to follow our hunches. John Macnicol pointed out to me that in both world wars full employment decimated the urban underclass, in both Britain and the United States. The stock magically became a flow. But there are warnings from America. Professor William Julius Wilson in Chicago does not share my qualms about the re-emergence of the underclass concept. He thinks that those of us who shy away from such terms 'fail to address one of the most important social transformations of recent history'.[7] He denies that the growth in poor families headed by women is due to some demoralising welfare factor and attributes it instead to the lack of employed men around as useful husbands. But his view and mine coalesce in seeing current theories about the growth of the underclass emerging simply because of the increase in urban unskilled unemployment, a factor completely outside the control of its victims.

I do not believe that any outside observer – beyond those skilful reporters, novelists and poets making imaginative leaps – really understands the time-consuming nature of modern poverty in a world where everything has its price, and where the most immediate worries are avoiding having the supply cut off by the electricity board. Of course the urban poor have to stick their children in front of the television, and of course they are obliged to buy the nearest available filling food. Inevitably, the poor pay more and get worse. This is so obvious a social fact that it needs no documentation. Every comparative index of deprivation shows that children reared in poor families suffer, not because of any lack of initiative or aspiration, not because of parental improvidence, but because everything has its price, and because that price is beyond reach.

There are several reasons why it is dangerous and socially destructive to categorise the city poor as a self-perpetuating underclass. The first is that it is not true. No long-term statistical research has actually followed a particular family long enough to justify such a claim. The children will keep wandering off into independence and out of the stigmatised group. The second is that it encourages an easy fatalism: the syndrome known as blaming the victims. Nothing, it is thought, can be done about these people at the bottom of the pile, so just cordon them off with vigilant policing and ignore them. The third is that it encourages fear: the underclass consists of young black predatory males, ready at any moment to take revenge on the society that rejects them. Maybe fear has its uses as an incentive for intelligent social action, but this particular fear perpetuates a grotesque and wounding racial stigma, and adds one more burden to the problems faced by the poor, non-academic urban young.

The prosaic truth is that the characteristic components of the inner city poverty stock are women, either old and trying to keep their homes together on pensions and social benefits, or middle-aged and trying to provide a family refuge for their dispirited adult offspring, or young but unsupported by male partners and struggling to rear children in conditions of endless disadvantage. Wander the streets of the poverty belt of any city and you are in the world of pram culture, as observed by Alexandra Artley:

> For a woman in King's Cross a pram or push-chair is her car. It conveys her young children, her plastic bags of shopping, takes bundles of dirty washing to the launderette, acts as an outdoor bed for the children and is used by them as a toy. As she may spend many hours waiting in DHSS or housing queues, children are strapped into it just to restrain them . . . Sometimes people take out an empty pram to convey a piece of furniture, a hopeless fridge, carpet, paraffin for oil heaters or bags of cat litter and potatoes . . .[8]

Dependent people abound, inside and outside the inner city. A civilised society could easily provide for their physical needs. What it ignores at its peril is the thirst for social and personal independence: the desire to get out of the stock and into the flow. So attention focuses on the newest generation. Criticism is directed at inner city schools, with little realisation of the problems of teaching in places where a dozen languages are spoken but, more importantly, where there is a widespread feeling that schooling has not met felt needs. David Donnison stressed to me that the most productive learning experiences in his particular patch of the city took place when people 'with an agenda of their own, sought help with problems they defined for themselves . . . none of it was done by people officially described as "teachers" '.

The most impressive of these city out-of-school educators is Chris Webb, a former teacher who is contemptuous of the idea of the existence of an urban underclass. He was appointed in 1974 to run the privately funded Notting Dale Urban Studies Centre, charged with the task of exploring the ways in which the urban environment itself could be used as an educational medium. He succeeded remarkably well in making it possible for the centre's findings to become a spur for local parents to gain some degree of control over their surround-ings and to change them in certain, if limited, ways.[9] He realised the limitations of this approach. What could it really mean for the disaffected young who would rather be somewhere else? So at Notting Dale he initiated a 'community technology centre', aiming to give the new sophisticated computer skills to the very inner city school-leavers who had been criticised for their failure to acquire them. He says, 'We opened our doors and were filled with young black people with about four CSEs. Everyone thought it would fail, but it was an enormous success.'

This achievement was indeed incredibly successful, and has been widely imitated. It is an immensely important contribution to the discussion of stock and flow in the city underclass. But there are other routes out of the cruel and complacent stereotype. One is the enjoyable irony that the alleged ghetto culture has made its own inroads into the entertainment industry – in music, drama, poetry and dance. Its exemplars have moved from stock into flow, confident in their own exuberant ability. Another is the achievement of some poor, young, unemployed inner city dwellers to make the same transition, once they have been given the opportunity to rehouse themselves and gain skills at the same time. This will be discussed in Chapter 10.

But the truth is that the hard work of helping people out of the undifferentiated pool of the alleged underclass rests with those people whom Ray Pahl called 'the pragmatic realists who know in their practical hearts that in the end piecemeal amelioration will be called in to do the job'. They include a huge variety of self-generated groups, impenetrable to the outsider, which are based on religious or ethnic origins and are formed to keep a language, faith or culture alive, to provide credit unions to keep people out of the hands of loan sharks, or to preserve musical, theatrical or dance traditions. They are not called in; they simply arise in any community. They are wise enough to seize any funding made available to inner city cultures, even though often their only demand is for cheap rentable premises.

If there was only one single measure, however, which outside bodies could make to change the situation of the alleged urban underclass, it would be the insertion of a vast expansion of nursery education. There is not the slightest doubt that some city children are at a disadvantage from the moment they are born, and that the earliest years of education are the most important. An exhaustive survey of young children in Inner London found that the strongest predictor of attainment at the age of 7 was 'the amount of 3R knowledge that the children had before they ever started school'.[10] Perhaps the biggest contribution that could be made to moving the stock into flow would be a squad of under-cover nursery teachers disguised as child-minders.

CHAPTER 9

THE BATTLE FOR COIN STREET

In the 1950s the writer V. S. Pritchett evoked the city he had grown up in with a book called *London Perceived*, about the meaning of the place, beyond the royal city, the ceremonial city, the shopping city or the tourist city. Two decades later, when it fell to him to revise his text he did so with a lamentation: 'I could not know that in a year or two of publication my text would become an epitaph on the death of the Victorian city with its lovely, low, almost Venetian skyline and the daily passing of those intimacies which had given the place its distinction as the most liveable and amiable capital in Europe.'[1]

He had been brought up in South London. His first job was in the leather trade in Bermondsey and he had learned to understand the intricate network of homes and jobs that held the city together. So it was with a certain anguish that he reported in the mid-1970s that 'The sober and various graces of that London are now being wiped out by the rapacity of property developers and the megalomania of the engineers whose ideal is the standard high-rise American or West German prison block and its exercise yards, the destruction of locality, the paralysis of traffic, whose real ambition is to make quick fortunes out of renting the sky.'[2]

Every Londoner knows the truth of this comment. In the immediate postwar years, the area next to County Hall was cleared for the Festival of Britain, celebrating the centenary of the Great Exhibition of 1851 and signalling Britain's entry into the era of new hopes and opportunities. The then London County Council (LCC) was buying up a multitude of sites on the South Bank of the Thames, east of County Hall, and building the Festival Hall, and subsequently the other halls and galleries, as well as the National Theatre, in what is now known as the South Bank Arts Centre. Today, as the concert-goers and playgoers go home, the spaces beneath them are colonised by the homeless.

These areas were part of Pritchett's 'low, almost Venetian skyline', but of course, seen close-up, were the usual riverside jumble of wharves, factories and warehouses, and small streets of houses, shops and schools, neglected for generations and battered in the war. The only landmarks were the Shot Tower (preserved for a while in deference to public sentiment) and the Oxo Tower (cherished because Londoners were amused by the way its owners had circumvented a ban on advertising by having windows which accidentally formed their trade mark).

The LCC went on acquiring sites on the south side of the river, with no very clear idea of what to do with them but with a certain foresight in view of the subsequent escalation of land prices. The big warehouses (Boots, W.H. Smith's, HMSO) moved on. But there was a solid core of residents in those neglected little streets, people with humble city jobs who needed to live in central areas because they started work long before the commuters had arrived.

In the decades of neglect, when nobody was interested in them or their homes, everything went slowly downhill. Old inhabitants remember not only the market stalls and corner shops, but also a whole series of multiple retailers who thought that their custom was worth while (like David Greig, Maypole Dairy, Lipton's, and Home & Colonial), as well as schools, pubs and clubs – everything from the children's dental clinic to Cook's Basket Shop with its wickerwork boxing kangaroo.

For decades the main income-generating industry of the area became clearing the sites for car parking. The surviving residents found its emptiness dangerous and menacing. It had turned into a land bank, a commodity like gold in a vault: too valuable to be useful. But today you can look over the river from the Embankment on the north side and see, on the right, the National Theatre and Kent House (the tower occupied by London Weekend Television) and, on your left, Kings Reach Tower. Between them the long empty space has become a reconstruction of that 'low, almost Venetian skyline' of roofs and trees, and beyond it you can actually see the buses in Stamford Street, passing the London Nautical School.

In the foreground, there is that well-known Oxo Tower, dwarfed by its neighbour at Kings Reach (intended to be a hotel but now just another office complex), and the tower carries a huge placard saying 'Welcome to Coin Street: Homes and Jobs: A Community Victory'. Behind that slogan is a story of immense complexity, related less to the merits of the case for low-rent housing rather than office development, than to the nature of the left–right divide in London

politics. The one-time LCC was replaced by the Greater London
Council (GLC), which before its abolition was alternatively led by the
Conservative Party and the Labour Party, and the boundary between
the London boroughs of Lambeth and Southwark runs in an
arbitrary way across the Coin Street site.

Members of the Association of Waterloo Groups, a federation of
local bodies drawn together by the fact that everyone seemed to be
against them, explained to me the daunting history of their struggle.
The 13 acres between Waterloo and Blackfriars bridges had mostly
been acquired by the LCC in the 1950s. The Heron Corporation was
granted planning permission for one of the sites for a big hotel,
though it was never built, nor was their proposal for an even larger
one in 1974. By that time the local groups had persuaded Lambeth
Council that the area should be used for housing and a public park.
The central government and the GLC gave their approval to these
schemes, but after the 1977 elections the GLC dropped the housing
plans which its architects had prepared for three of the eight sites, and
backed projects for hotels and offices from the Heron Corporation
and from Commercial Properties, owned by the Vestey family.
Together with Southwark Council, the GLC also supported a rival
scheme submitted by Greycoat Estates, a firm dominated by the
McAlpine family.

In 1979 a six-month-long public inquiry was held by the
Department of the Environment into both these proposals and into
the housing promoted by Lambeth Council. In the following year,
Michael Heseltine, Secretary of State for the Environment, announced
that he would not grant permission for the 'massive and over-
dominant' office proposals, nor for the housing plans which 'failed to
exploit the employment potential of the sites'. By the end of 1980, the
rival developers joined together to form Greycoat Commercial
Estates and their new proposal was opposed by community groups. A
public inquiry was opened and then adjourned in view of the GLC
elections of 1981. Just before the elections, the GLC sold key parts of
the site to Greycoat Commercial Estates. The inquiry ended in 1982
and in the following year the secretary of state announced that he
supported planning consent for both schemes.

Policy decisions do not totally coincide with party assumptions,
and the problem for the local groups was that of tackling a variety of
politicians at every level of government to make the elementary point
that the area should be redeveloped both to generate local jobs and as
housing and public open space, rather than as offices or hotels. Steve
Barran, a toolroom turner and grinder by trade, stressed that

The work I do is done in a small workshop, by a workforce of less than a dozen people. Not so many years ago this area was full of such small workshops providing employment – and service – to the community, here and at large. Now there are almost none and all those jobs have disappeared. Why? Because the sites those workshops stood on were worth more as office development land. And yet a community needs those kinds of employment if it is to remain alive and healthy.[3]

His view was sustained by the Inspector in his report on one of the endless public inquiries into planning applications for the site. He commented that

There is a very high rate of unemployment in Lambeth and Southwark, coupled with a serious mismatch between the few jobs on offer and the skills available; a clear distinction must be made between the number of jobs a scheme may generate and how many of these jobs will be new ones that will actually give work to someone who is unemployed . . . Both North Southwark and North Lambeth have increasingly vulnerable and declining populations; their viability in terms of supporting schools, shops and other vital services has reached a critical threshold, as has their morale in struggling against the odds . . .

The Inspector was also moved to say: 'I have great admiration for the self-help and determination practised by the Waterloo Community; their root need is for homes, particularly family homes, whereby the community can be strengthened and consolidated and given grounds for a belief in the future . . .'[4] His tribute to their stamina and persistence was certainly earned. A handful of people with no institutional backing had struggled for years against one speculative proposal after another. With the secretary of state's approval given to both the Community Plan *and* to that of Greycoat Commercial Estates, a stalemate of extraordinary complexity had been reached. By this time the Association of Waterloo Groups was supported by the GLC and by both Lambeth and Southwark councils, who went to the High Court and the Court of Appeal, arguing that the approval for the Greycoat proposal was not legal. They lost. But then, prompted perhaps by the prospect of yet more planning inquiries or by changes in the property market, Greycoat Commercial Estates and the associated companies withdrew. They sold back their interests in the site to the GLC for £2,700,000.

That body itself was on the verge of extinction and, 24 hours before the government's legislation to control the GLC's financial activities, it disposed of the site. Part of the land was leased for 125 years for £1 to the Society for Co-operative Dwellings and the freehold of the rest was sold to a newly formed non-profit company, Coin Street Community Builders, for £750,000. This transaction was presented in the press as an example of the bizarre prodigality of the GLC. It was, in fact, sanctioned by the district valuer and reflected the effect of planning permission on land valuation. The 'value' of the site as housing at fair rents, as public open space, and for all the other socially useful aspects of the intentions of the Association of Waterloo Groups, was infinitely less than its 'value' as offices.

Coin Street Community Builders, chaired by Fred Miller, a lifelong Waterloo resident, took over the plans prepared by the North Southwark Community Development Group and the Association of Waterloo Groups. These include 400 houses to be let at fair rents to people in housing need from the two boroughs, a new park and an extension of the South Bank Riverside Walk, shops and a light industrial workshops development intended to provide up to 1,200 jobs. The housing will be owned and managed by the tenants in seven separate housing co-operatives.

The Mulberry Housing Co-operative, first of the seven, was opened by Sir George Young in October 1988, two years after, as junior environment minister, he had sanctioned the scheme. It is built in the form of a hollow square, with small private gardens leading into a communal space – the pattern developed in the nineteenth century in Holland Park. It has all those qualities we now seek in housing: quiet unassertiveness, urbanity and domesticity.

It was an emotional moment for the veterans who had seen local and national governments, ministers, policies, promises and property developers come and go over the past 15 years, and had seen the area itself allowed to fall into dereliction ever since the war. For the minister's approval in 1986, as Tim Roberts remarked at the time, 'marks the end of one of the most concerted long-running and on occasions bitter planning battles ever seen. But it also signals something much more significant: the victory by well-organised, well-briefed and well-motivated local people in the face of seemingly insurmountable odds.'[5]

The battle may be over, but in my experience people are unable to discuss even Coin Street's restoration of the 'low, almost Venetian skyline' without reference to the party politics behind its inception. This is unfortunate because the Coin Street saga raises two fundamental questions: What is a city for? And who is entitled to live there? I am reminded of an incident which Ray Gosling told me about. He was interviewing citizens of Chester, among the boutiques and wine bars of The Rows in the centre of that city. 'But where do the poor people live?' he asked. 'Oh, out there', he was told, an arm pointing in the general direction of the Lache Estate on the fringe of the city. 'We call them the Reservations.'

No one has yet been willing to tell me to my face that people with low incomes and no chance of a mortgage have no right to occupy valuable space in the city. The Victorians were more forthright. In 1855 Charles Pearson, solicitor to the City Corporation, asked the Select Committee on Metropolitan Communications 'whether it is not monstrous that commercial men should be tolerating a system where the poor are living upon ground that is worth £750 an acre per annum, when they might be transferred nightly in 20 minutes and back again to land that is to be obtained for £200 per acre'.[6]

The implications of this argument were to stay with us for a century or more. The LCC, for example, rehoused countless families in the 1930s at Becontree and Dagenham, only to find that nutritional standards actually declined as a greater proportion of the family income was spent on travelling to work.[7] The situation was only reversed by the arrival of local industry.

But the ultimate triumph of the founder-members of the housing co-operatives at Coin Street (dear old residents like Doreen Ramsay and Fred Miller, who were not themselves the beneficiaries of their hard work) was to establish that, given an appropriate manipulation of site valuation and given access to the long-term credit that more affluent city dwellers take for granted, poor people *can* house themselves.

I have lived long enough to witness the transitory triumphs of a host of rival ideologies in city housing. When I was young the advocates of comprehensive redevelopment rejoiced that bombing had provided opportunities that would not have arisen in decades of slum clearance. When they ran out of bomb sites, following the ideology of 'raze and rise', they created their own blighted areas, destined for eventual total renewal.

There were always protesters, but they were ignored. Frederic Osborn, for example, wrote in 1945:

I don't think philanthropic housing people anywhere realise the irresistible strength of the impulse towards the family house and garden as prosperity increases; they think the suburban trend can be reversed by large-scale multi-storey buildings in the down-town districts, which is not only a pernicious belief from the human point of view, but a delusion . . . In a few years, the multi-storey method will peter out . . . Damage will be done to society by the trial; but probably all I can do is to hasten the date of disillusion. If I have underestimated the complacency of the urban masses, the damage may amount to a disaster.[8]

The damage *did* amount to a disaster, as city dwellers can testify. But throughout the 1940s, 1950s and 1960s nobody cared to listen. Even in the 1970s, when the cash was still swilling around in the bran-tub, the authorities continued to ignore those who pointed out that drawing a line on a map in town and county halls (verified by a clerk in the passenger seat of a moving car, ticking off the house numbers so that the closure orders could be correctly addressed) to decide the fate of the city dwellers' housing led to an absurd paradox. For, while on one side of that line, whole streets were selected for demolition as being unfit for human habitation, on the other side absolutely identical houses, previously blighted by the prospect of a decade of redevelopment, were slowly beginning their upward spiral into the sought-after end of the housing market, aided by the merry whirr of Black and Deckers.

It is instructive to compare the bizarre prices that the rescued houses fetch today with the sad condition of the new estates which were built opposite. Graham Lomas, former deputy strategic planner for the GLC, reached the conclusion 15 years ago that in London more fit houses had been destroyed since the war by public authorities than had been replaced.[9] The urge to demolish had outstripped the capacity to build, and the same devastating phenomenon was to be found in other British cities, such as Liverpool and Glasgow. Even worse, in its effect on tenants, was the fact that housing management had moved further and further from the occupants, and that maintenance had become so remote and expensive that it slowly ceased to happen at all.[10]

It was inevitable, rather than surprising, that the pendulum of opinion should have swung against the direct provision of rented housing by local authorities. There have been plenty of suggestions for rescuing council housing from the paternalism and bureaucratic remoteness of its providers, with a range of possibilities: local management, tenant participation and tenant control.[11] Political leaders of both major parties failed to grasp the urgency of the task. The situation of the people at the bottom of the pile became more and more desperate. Current politicians simply ignore not only the destitute people living rough, whose plight is often the simple fact of family breakdown rather than personal deficiencies, but also employed people hanging on to a low-paid job as an alternative to unemployment and quite unable to find a slot in the housing market. Likewise, they pay no attention to the plight of those trapped in the ludicrously expensive horrors of bed-and-breakfast accommodation, when the sums paid on their behalf by local authorities could pay for the homeless to house themselves.

Coin Street is a special case. Because of the absurdities of financial speculation in land in central London, it was an absolute challenge to accepted ideas about who is allowed to live in the city centre. Fortunately, in British cities there are a whole series of small but outstandingly successful examples of people on low incomes housing themselves and, in doing so, literally changing their lives. They ought to be acceptable on both sides of the political divide because they exemplify 'dweller-control' (something taken totally for granted by the owner-occupier) as the first principle of housing. The following chapter describes a few of these successful adventures.

CHAPTER 10

CITY PEOPLE *CAN* HOUSE THEMSELVES

For half a lifetime I knew the city of Glasgow as the largest housing authority in Europe, but I also knew that it was the most paternalistic. Even when it did desirable and sensible things, it did them in an incredibly heavy-handed way. A tenant once explained to me how she came home from work one day and found a tree in her garden. This was a great gesture from the corporation's parks department, worthy of emulation everywhere, except for the crucial fact that nobody had thought it important to tell her. On enquiry she learned that it had been decided that trees should be planted in every other garden, and hers was one of these.

Faced with the bankruptcy of traditional housing policy, the city has experienced a painful and partial change of heart with results that anyone can go and see. The machinery of local government has slowly engineered the opportunity for its tenants to take control of their own housing. One of a dozen tenants to explain the meaning of this was Frances McCall of Calvay Co-operative Ltd in Glasgow, who was also chairwoman of the Scottish Federation of Housing Co-operatives. She had lived in Calvay Road for 20 years, brought up her family there, and had watched the decline of both the environment and of employment, and the consequent loss of hope. She says that

> . . . unemployment is considerably larger than Glasgow's average; the permanently sick and disabled proportion of this population is relatively high; the labour forces are largely unskilled; there are few work opportunities in the general area – in fact there are none; they have got three shops; the area is deteriorating at an alarming rate; and it's a hard-to-let area . . . When your area becomes a hard-to-let area then you get a stigma attached to you, because if you want to rent a television, or

something, and you give your address, they go: 'Oh, no, no, I'm sorry, you can't have that. That's a bad area you stay in.' So I'm glad to say that there are groups of initiatives in Glasgow where people are saying: 'I live in a bad area but I am going to do something about it.'[1]

The big change in Glasgow began falteringly when, in the late 1970s, the city decided to sponsor a new estate, Summerston, as a co-operative, and even this venture was beset with problems, simply because, like everything else, it was imposed from above. It won through in the end and, in the early 1980s, Glasgow tenants (through the medium of the Association of Community Technical Aid Centres and the Scottish Tenant Participation Advisory Service) began to visit Liverpool and the new initiatives happening there. Then the council's experiments in tenant management had a jolt from the Scottish Office's arbitrary decisions on capital allocation for modernisation. Central government decided that the sum the city would be allowed to spend on its own housing in 1984/85 was to be reduced from £72 million to £49 million, while the sum allocated to other sectors, housing only a third of the population, was increased from £54 million to £77 million.[2]

Glasgow District Council responded with a proposal to sell thousands of homes to community ownership co-operatives. Johnston Birchall explained the convolutions of intervention and circumvention that this entailed:

But what can co-ops possibly do about such a disastrous situation, except shoulder a responsibility which no one in their right minds would take on? It is not so wild a suggestion as it seems at first sight. Co-ops, as non-public forms of social ownership, are eligible to tap into considerable funds which Glasgow holds, but which the Conservative government will only allow to be spent on the private housing sector. They can apply for private finance to buy the dwellings and for council grants to improve them. Nor is the plan as opportunistic as it seems; the new type of co-op fits into an existing strategy of maximising the use of stock by improving housing management and tenant participation . . . The studies showed that viability hinged on low acquisition costs from the council, improvement and environmental grants and promotional grants to set the co-ops up, low-start building society loans with tax relief on the interest, and government loan guarantees.[3]

There was intense opposition from the Scottish Office, but support
from another government agency, the Housing Corporation. After
years of argument, some of the Glasgow co-operatives have come
into being and are flourishing.

In Liverpool the movement for housing co-operatives began in the
early 1970s as a buy-out from private landlords who had shown
themselves unwilling or unable to rehabilitate their streets of
substandard housing. Thanks to the existence of secondary co-
operatives set up to steer members through the quagmires of
incomprehensible legislation, and thanks to the disillusionment with
council rehousing policy, the demand grew for newly built housing
co-operatives for poorly housed citizens. Several groups took the
plunge into the long adventure of finding a site, commissioning an
architect, working out a design and gaining finance (Liverpool City
Council or the Housing Corporation). Discussing the first of these
co-operatives, the *Architects' Journal's* correspondent, Nick Wates,
stressed the huge significance of the venture:

> Something incredible has happened in Liverpool – arguably the
> most important step forward in British housing for decades.
> Without anyone else in the country really noticing it, an era
> spanning sixty years of paternalistic public housing provision
> has quietly come to an end. In its place a new way of building
> publicly funded housing has taken over in which the users are
> firmly in the driving seat.[4]

The experience of the members of the Weller Street[5] and Hesketh
Street[6] co-operatives is fully documented. One of the difficulties they
had to face was the continually changing policy of the city council
under a series of political regimes: Labour, Liberal, Liberal/
Conservative, and finally Labour (Militant). The last-named of these
actually took over co-operative designed housing (the Good
Neighbours Housing Co-operative) and turned it into old-style
council housing. Caught in the political crossfire was one of the most
ambitious of all the Liverpool co-operatives, the Eldonian Community Association. Its chairman, Tony McGann, stresses that
community building is not only about housing:

> I know co-operatives, people in housing associations, they do a
> great job, but then you get people who think, well, we've got a
> housing co-operative, and that's the end of it. That's far from the
> end of it. You have got to get involved in everything that's

connected with your community, and with everyone who is going to make a decision about your community. You take the Eldonians, for instance. We're involved in about fifteen to twenty-five different initiatives. Because of the unemployment of that area, we've now decided to tackle that. And we've started up, or attempted to start up, small businesses, worker's co-ops, a horticultural project; we're involved with the community programme, we're converting an old warehouse into a sports centre . . .[7]

Like everyone else in the movement for dweller-control in housing, Tony McGann stressed to me the huge growth of self-confidence it gives to people who have been pushed around all their lives. This is why Alan Hoyte, the first chairman of the Hesketh Street Co-operative, said that 'In general, in Liverpool, people are told what they are getting, not asked what they want. But once we had established our viability by being accepted by the government for funding, we determined everything; the way we lived, and who we employed to run our affairs. We did not succumb to the bureaucracy.'

Anyone who has watched Liverpool and its governmental machinery in the decades since the war, and has watched the city's awesome economic decline, has been aghast at the way its politicians of every party have endlessly ignored observable realities. At the time when jobs in the port were being lost daily, they were proclaiming it as Europe's Atlantic City, proposing vast new roads and a £10 million civic centre, and ploughing up 450 acres of old housing. Back in the 1970s, my mental image of the city's planning officer showed him desperately and unavailingly crying 'Stop!' in front of the bulldozer piloted by what Mike Franks called 'the unholy alliance of the medical officer of health, the city engineer, the housing architect and the town clerk, all working together to implement the wishes of their politicians'.[8] I concluded that

A besetting fault of Liverpool's administration, whether we are thinking of its elected representatives or their employees is that it has failed to take its electorate seriously. The citizens have been seen as feckless though lovable children whose aspirations and initiatives, though understandable, were not susceptible of incorporation in the official reality.[9]

Yet Liverpool is a city where one little local initiative after another, starved of funds and premises, sought to provide alternatives in schooling, playgrounds, youth employment and training, even a broadcasting station called Radio Doom. All these sparks of citizen self-assertion struggled against a sea of cynicism and public indifference before they finally came to fruition, just because it demands a long-term commitment on both sides – the funder and the user – in the field of co-operative housing. And as Tony McGann endlessly stresses, the experience of direct control by tenants can lead on to much more.

Hull, out on a limb on the other side of England, has suffered its own form of industrial decline. Its port is a shadow, its fishing a memory and its shipbuilding a ghost. Its biggest industry is education. One effect of its isolation and depression is that Victorian terraced houses, to which little has been done for decades, are still relatively cheap. Forty-seven per cent of the housing stock belongs to the council, yet at least 3,500 families are officially described as homeless, and this minimal figure ignores the young, single and footloose, and all those teenagers obliged to leave home after a marriage breakdown or a family row. In 1985 young, unemployed Reg Salmon borrowed enough in small loans from trusting friends to get a mortgage on a small house which together they set about renovating. With that house as security they got a bank loan to buy a second house. Then, with the help of Humberside Co-operative Development Agency, they set up a building co-operative, Giroscope Ltd, whose other directors were also under 25 and unemployed. The aims of the co-operative are 'the purchase, renovation, modernisation and furnishing of houses in a poor condition', and 'the renting out of these houses to unemployed people and to other disadvantaged groups such as single parents and disabled people'. By the end of 1988, the co-operative owned eight houses, accommodating about 30 young unemployed people and 4 children.

They explained to me how everything had improved as they gained skills, experience and credibility: 'The first house was a patch-up job and depended on mutual trust and robbing Peter to pay Paul, but we now find it easier to get loans and we have had grants from the Hull and East Riding Charitable Trust and from Charity Projects.' By now they had all acquired building skills and experience, as well as management know-how, and were in good standing with builders' merchants. A network of well-wishers advised them about cheap houses coming onto the market. They believe that once they have bought and renovated 20 houses their operation will be self-financing. They do not want to grow indefinitely and are willing to train people and to share their experience. They warn that, especially with the impact of new social security regulations on the homeless young, their precariously balanced budget would only work in those northern towns and cities where it is still possible to buy houses cheaply and put in a great deal of work. When I asked the co-operative members why their example had not been followed everywhere, they replied: 'It depends on three things. One is being willing to work very hard. Another is being willing to do it for very little money. And the third is the one that makes sense of the other two: a kind of political and social awareness.'

In Bristol, the Zenzele Self-Build Housing Association was formed by 12 unemployed young people, mostly black, unskilled and aged around 20. It was inspired by a local magistrate, Stella Clarke, and a steering group helped the members for two years to negotiate their way through the sources of finance. A site was obtained from the local authority with a provisional loan from the Housing Corporation. A very important agreement was won from the DHSS that the members could work on their two-storey block of 12 flats while continuing to draw social security payments. An individual mortgage for each member was provided by the Bristol and West Building Society and a general foreman was engaged to train the members and supervise the work.

It took 14 months for the members to build their flat, longer than expected, as some members got jobs and could only work in the evenings and at weekends. All the members eventually found work, mostly as a result of the skills they had acquired. Zenzele set several precedents and has inspired several other ventures. In Birmingham, for example, Abdul Bahar of the Neejesshow Self Build Housing Association says: 'We visited the Zenzele scheme and were inspired by what we saw. We came away thinking, those people did something, so why can't we? This will be the first activity of its kind in the Bengali community – it hasn't happened before because we lacked information and proper advice.' He explained that

We are living in overcrowded conditions and are unemployed because our skills – mostly in the heavy engineering field – are no longer required. We are hardworking people – people from the Bengali community used to working from seven in the morning until seven at night in engineering factories and foundries – that is one of the reasons I'm so sure that the project will work.[10]

A number of the original Zenzele builders have moved on. They have married and needed bigger homes, or they have taken jobs elsewhere. And, of course, they have sold at a profit. I was disconcerted to find a number of people in the housing world criticising Zenzele for this reason and urging that the flats should have been for rent rather than for sale, so as to keep them available for people outside the normal housing market. It worried me that poor people should have to be the bearers of the social conscience of a nation whereas owner-occupation and the advantages that accrue from it are taken for granted by the majority. I raised the matter with Chris Gordon, a Zenzele member who is now secretary of the Bristol Self Build Development Agency. He mildly observed that the Zenzele group had put three and a half years of their lives into housing themselves. Ray Gosling made the same point to me far more strongly. 'Everyone tut-tuts about the Underclass', he said, 'and when people who start out with nothing become people with something we put them in the same category as the sharp ones who start with everything.'

The feasibility of poor people being enabled to house themselves rests in practice on a range of continually changing fiscal and administrative issues. One is the availability of land outside the ordinary speculative market. Another is the attitude of the Department of Social Security, and a third, simply to make use of loopholes in the rules, is the valuation put on the builders' own labour.[11] Yet another is the question of access to the kind of information provided by advice centres in order to steer people through the thickets of legislation and administration.[12] A final point that has to be made is that there is no particular virtue in sweat. In those parts of the world where self-building is the normal procedure for the great mass of the population, it is normal and natural to use the special skills of neighbours and friends and to recompense them. When I asked Michael Barraclough of the Great Eastern Self Build Housing Association what happened if a member was suddenly thrown out of work and consequently had more time and less money, he instantly replied, 'Naturally they'd tumble over themselves to employ him or her on the site.'

The importance of self-building is as a means rather than an end, although, as anyone who has ever met a self-builder knows, it generates immense pride and self-confidence among people who have housed themselves that way. The most remarkable illustration of this came from the Lewisham Self-Build Housing Society in South London which based its approach on the work of the late Walter Segal, an architect who had slowly evolved a system of low-cost, lightweight, but high-quality house construction. He did not see himself as providing solutions to the 'housing problem'. In fact he remarked in 1971 that 'It sounds absurd that one should try to search for methods of building cheaply when we have the impossible problem of accelerating land cost and do nothing about it.'[13] He was right, of course, but his approach, as applied in Lewisham, was an inspiration: 'Single-handedly, Segal invented the impossible idea of ordinary, non-skilled working-class women and men from the waiting list for public authority housing, building their own homes. Lewisham self-builders have ranged from retired men in the 60s to single mothers; many are families with young children who constructively joined in creating their own homes.'[14]

The members of the group were, by one vote in the borough council, given the chance to house themselves on sites which were thought to be too small or too awkward for the council to use itself. It took years of argument with the planners, the district surveyor and even the Inland Revenue to allow it to happen, yet members of the group have told me, quite simply, that the experience completely changed their lives. Brian Richardson, as housing architect for the London Borough of Lewisham at the time, was the enabler for the self-builders and I know he was not exaggerating when he said:

From being dissatisfied tenants putting up with bad housing because there was no hope of anything better for people in their circumstances, they became transformed by their own actions. Deeds of daring, marathons of effort, triumphs of skill and ingenuity were performed by individuals on their own and working together which they had no idea they were capable of before.[15]

This is a universal experience among poor city dwellers who have actually been able to control their own housing destiny. The question to be asked is why, everywhere, have we put such a mountain of obstacles in their way?

CHAPTER 11

CAN THEY MAKE JOBS TOO? THE ITALIAN LESSON

If only we had the will, and the willingness, to invest in people rather than in property, we could, as the last chapter shows, make huge improvements in the housing prospects of inner city dwellers. The employment situation is far more intractable. My intention is to suggest that there are important lessons to be absorbed from the recent experience of the industrial cities of northern Italy.

I once met a pleasant young man who at last had found himself a job delivering Egg-o-grams. His friend and employer had the bright idea that instead of Kiss-o-grams (where some poor young woman, desperate for work, was hired to deliver a kiss to a stranger on his birthday), a message could be rolled up small and pushed into a blown egg. The eggs themselves could be instantly decorated with felt-tip pens, following attractive Easter traditions.

This young man was thus a contemporary hero. He had removed himself from the culture of dependency, no longer needed to rely on social benefits, and had therefore joined the enterprise culture. Taxpayers were thus relieved of the burden of supporting him. Moralists would find his case to be yet another example of our irrational preference for private affluence over public squalor, for if he had applied to the local authority for a job in cleaning the environment, or attending to the needs of the old or disabled, he would undoubtedly have been told that central government had obliged the council to reduce, rather than increase, its labour force.

The irony of current trends in public employment has been well described by Peter Hall, who notes that if there is pressure to cut costs,

> ... the inevitable result is the decline of certain services which are among the oldest and most basic functions of local authorities,

such as the upkeep of the streets; hence all those potholes and pavement cracks. The paradox thus emerges that these services are now actually worse than they were when we were much poorer and local government was much slimmer. And these happen to be just the ones on which the quality of our common civic life so much depends.[1]

The terrible irony is that when the humblest of environmentally useful jobs might have helped people who had been thrown out of work by the collapse of traditional employment in the 1970s and 1980s, they have ceased to exist. This is why it is useful to suggest that the experience of unemployment in British cities has been the opposite of that in their Italian counterparts. The same world trends have affected both, but the results have been very different.

Between 1960 and 1981 major conurbations lost 1.7 million of the 2.1 million manufacturing jobs lost in Britain as a whole . . . Government policies, together with increasingly competitive external conditions, have led to the closure of capacity and widespread redundancies. At a broader level restrictive macro-economic policies contributed substantially to the collapse of output in the economy in the early 1980s and to the sudden rise in unemployment: 1.2 million jobs were lost in manufacturing between 1980 and 1982 alone.[2]

By 1985 London itself 'could claim the dubious distinction of having the largest concentration of unemployed people in the advanced industrial world. In relative terms, however, the great northern cities like Manchester, Liverpool and Newcastle were much worse off.'[3]

Small business was ignored for decades by politicians and economists in spite of a revealing government report many years ago which saw the small-firm sector as 'the traditional breeding-ground for new industries – that is for innovation writ large' and noted that technical change could make small-scale operation highly economic, but recorded that 'In manufacturing, the share of small firms in employment and output has fallen substantially and almost continuously since the mid-1920s.'[4] The devastating loss of industrial jobs in the 1970s and 1980s led to a sudden surge of interest and solicitude about the small firm. Experts on the actual prospects of small business watched the process with a certain sardonic amusement. In the words of David Watkins and his colleagues from the Manchester Business School:

Both major political parties subscribed through the sixties and into the seventies to a view of industry which broadly speaking, believed that bigger was better. Economies of scale in production, finance and markets were sought in the belief that only through the creation of organisations of a size to be internationally competitive would British industry continue to thrive in world markets. The key political questions revolved more around the ownership and control of the commanding heights of British industry, which were to bring continued growth and prosperity, than to their creation and development . . . but it has become clear that the commanding heights look both less formidable and less attractive than they once did. Many have been scaled by foreign climbers; some famous peaks have succumbed to earthquakes . . . Small wonder that so many vested interests see new challenges in the foothills.

They also warned that we would be disappointed if we believed that more than a small percentage of the then 3 million unemployed could be 'redeployed in the short term, even with extensive retraining. One can at best hope for small miracles from small firms.'[5]

Nevertheless, a series of central and local government measures sought to give new encouragement to small business. The most interesting of these have been among the humblest. The Enterprise Allowance scheme was initiated to avoid the absurdity of unemployed people being prosecuted for fraud if they continued to draw unemployment pay when they first attempted to set up their own businesses. Quite often, at a minimal cost to the public purse, it has worked. The difference between social security payments and the year's Enterprise Allowance is so small that even failure costs little, however disheartening for the individual. Several people among those who failed, as well as those who succeeded, have told me of its great value as a learning experience about self-employment, its pitfalls and potentialities.

The other interesting and suggestive venture is the community workshop. This is not part of any employment-creating policy, but a local initiative set up in several cities by people who have perceived that one of the deprivations experienced by the poor is lack of space and of access to tools. Since every city has vacant buildings, they sought a place with access to light and power, where workbenches and machinery could be installed and expertise brought in to enable people to undertake their own motor repairs, furniture construction, toy-making and so on. Funding has been found from local authorities, charitable sources or the government's Community Programme. Such ventures have often been a boon to unemployed people picking up new skills. The rules usually preclude the use of the premises for money-earning ventures. Fortunately, the ruling is often ignored. Everyone concerned with such ventures is convinced of their value and potential. But the government abruptly announced that with the introduction of its Employment Training scheme, the Community Programme funding would end. All Community Programme projects, including some community workshops, were offered the opportunity to convert to Employment Training, but about 45 per cent of them were unable or unwilling to do so, or could not find a way of conforming with the Employment Training rules.

In Britain we have been singularly unsuccessful in finding replacements for those city industrial jobs that have been lost. It is vaguely assumed, just as it has been in the 'revitalisation' of American cities, that the new commercial, financial and tourist developments will create a trickle-down of service occupations. So it does, but at wages too low to support current urban rents. The secretary of the US Department of Housing and Urban Development displayed a singular lack of familiarity with the catering trade by suggesting that many a great chef had started as a dishwasher.[6] Everywhere you go in the industrial cities of Britain and the United States you see vast ruined or empty factories and a variety of our current desperate alternatives to industry: garden festivals, conference centres, shopping malls, theme parks and aquariums or museums of our industrial heritage. Anything, in fact – including Kiss-o-grams – except the opportunity to become involved in either socially useful or productive work.

The experience of Italy is different, and it made me think back to Lewis Mumford's eulogy, mentioned in Chapter 2, of Kropotkin's examination of *Fields, Factories and Workshops*. Mumford remarked that

> Kropotkin foresaw what many big corporations were to discover only during the Second World War; namely, that even when total assemblage was a big one, the farming out of special industrial operations in 'bits and pieces' actually often made the reputed economies of concentrated large-scale organisation, the industrial tendency that justified other forms of metropolitan bigness, dubious. The finer the technology, the greater the need for the human initiative and skill conserved in the small workshop. Effective transportation and fine organisation were

often superior to the mere physical massing of plant under one roof.[7]

I single out this observation from 1961 on a book first published in 1899 simply because I have searched in vain in the literature of British industrial technology or management to find a similar insight. The effects of this kind of perception were probably unexpected in Italy too, for an American study of Italian industry and its significance for the rest of the world explains that

> What happened next caught managers, trade unions, workers, and government officials by surprise, although it had been foreshadowed in Prato and elsewhere . . . The Brescian mini-mills moved at least as fast as their American counterparts in continuous casting; the farm- and construction-equipment industry in Emilia-Romagna got into production of sophisticated hydraulic-control devices . . . Wage levels in areas such as Emilia-Romagna (where there were virtually no large firms and a proliferation of small shops) drew even with the levels in Piedmont, the most industrialised Italian region. Similarly, unemployment rates fell . . . A dramatic sign of the prosperity of the new small-firm sector was the rise of Modena – the capital of the decentralised economy – in the rank list of provincial wealth . . .[8]

I cite these authoritative findings because I was almost resigned to the British view, shared by the political left and right, that there was something inevitable about the death of British industry, while even for me the Kropotkinian revolution in scale was only to come at some time in the future. Certainly, the largest empty factory I have ever seen was the vast kilometre-long FIAT building at Lingotto in Turin. One small part of it has been rehabilitated as a conference centre, but there the resemblance to our British industrial graveyards ends. For the taxi-driver who drove me around (a former FIAT employee, needless to say), also drove me to the new industrial suburbs filled with hundreds of tiny workshops. There, former employees sub-contract on their own account – not only for the new FIAT plant where cars are alleged to be 'hand-made by robots', but also for several other manufacturers – or simply make products of their own for which they have found a market. Even in the very centre of Turin you come across dozens of small workshops in all the metal trades. There are several ways of interpreting the transformation of Italian industry. Some observers see the process of dispersal as the ultimate triumph of international finance capital in breaking up the organised industrial proletariat: 'In the late 1960s labour militancy in many Italian industries reached levels that directly threatened firm profitability, and management undertook a series of strategies designed initially to reduce the disruptiveness of militant workers.'[9] This is certainly part of the truth. Since the strike of 1980, 60,000 workers have left FIAT. The regional secretary of the union CGIL, Pietro Marcenaro, told me that 'At that time nobody knew who won, but we now know that FIAT won.'

Others see the changes as inevitable and desirable. Richard Hatch of the Centre for Urban Reindustrialisation Studies in New Jersey sees it in exactly the same terms as Lewis Mumford's account of Kropotkin's vision. He explains that

It is based on a large number of very small, flexible enterprises that depend on broadly skilled workers and multiple-use automated machinery. Essentially intermediate producers, they link together in varying combinations and patterns to perform complex manufacturing tasks for widening markets. These firms combine rapid innovation with a high degree of democracy in the workplace.

He also stresses the civic importance of this development: 'They tend to congregate in mixed-use neighbourhoods where work and dwelling are integrated. Their growth has been the objective of planning policy, architectural interventions, and municipal investment, with handsome returns in sustained economic growth and lively urban centres.'[10]

The late George Benello similarly found in the 'industrial renaissance' of north-eastern and central Italy 'a model that worked, creating in less than three decades, not hundreds but literally hundreds of thousands of small scale firms, out-producing conventionally run factories, and providing work which called forth skill, responsibility, and artistry from its democratically organised workforces'. He was

. . . amazed at the combination of sophisticated design and production technology with human scale work-life, and by the extent and diversity of integrated and collaborative activity within this network. Small cities, such as Modena, had created 'artisan villages' – working neighbourhoods where production facilities and living quarters were within walking or bike range, where technical schools for the unemployed fed directly into newly created businesses, and where small firms using computerised techniques, banded together to produce complex products.[11]

These are large claims, but I saw plenty of evidence to support them. The first thing to surprise me about Ennio Mazzanti's workshop which I visited in Bologna was that his equipment must be worth hundreds of thousands of pounds. He told me that he had worked on the bench for 10 years in a motor-cycle factory and had then bought one lathe and one vertical milling machine to start up on his own. They still stand in a corner of the shop today, useful for one-off jobs. Now – using large, long-bed horizontal grinding machines (Swiss, German and British) – he and his son and three employees drill precision holes ('with a mirror finish', he explained) as subcontractors. The parts are then delivered and collected by the manufacturers. 'But suppose they go to another, cheaper, specialist?' I asked. 'That doesn't bother me', he replied. 'I work for five different firms and can always pick up more jobs.' If the flow of long-run orders dried up, there would always be enough small jobs to pay off his bank loan (he expected each machine to be paid for in 10 years), and the overheads were low. He works a 10-hour day; his employees decide their own hours. He pays the same wage as any other engineering firm in Emilia-Romagna, and never has to worry about the paperwork which is done by computer equipment owned by a co-operative to which he subscribes.

There are reasons, of course, behind the astonishing way in which the small workshop economy has flourished. Whatever happens in the central government in Rome, there has always been agreement among the regional and city governments of northern Italy, and among all parties from the Communists to the Christian Democrats, to support small enterprise. In the 1950s the Cassa Artigiana was founded to provide credit below normal interest rates (at 1.5–2 per cent). There has been a continuity in this trend since the 1960s, with the result that a majority of employed workers are now in factories with fewer than 50 employees, and an increasing number in really tiny factories. They vary enormously. Some are traditional craft activities which have simply by-passed the industrial revolution and whose products are in great demand everywhere. Others follow the well-known sweatshop pattern where an entrepreneur hands out work to home-workers. They can be trapped in the system, or they might themselves be able to mechanise the process and earn a good living, aided by the availability of credit. Thus the owner of Essezeta, a small firm doing appliqué and speciality sewing for the knitwear industry, says 'I started with nothing. I used to work in a large firm. Then the business went bad and the factory closed. I had to take care of myself.' This woman in her late forties explained: 'I began with a simple machine, the kind of sewing machine you see at home. Then, step-by-step, I got real sewing machines and now I have electronic ones. I tell you these electronic machines give me a lot of pleasure.' She is now a fully equipped subcontractor like Mr Mazzanti, able to perform a particular operation for a variety of assemblers and manufacturers. Finally, there are those enterprises with a real degree of autonomy which find a market and produce finished goods themselves, like those in the textile industry around Carpi or the shoe firms of Rimini.

Thousands of these 'artisan shops' – defined in Italian legislation as those workshops with fewer than 22 workers and in which the owners themselves are engaged full-time – are jointly organised in co-operatively owned bodies like the Confederazione Nazionale dell' Artigianato (CNA) which in the province of Emilia-Romagna alone, apart from its concern with training and management, keeps the books of 60,000 firms and handles 120,000 payslips a month. It also handles export marketing and guarantees credit for members, operating as a loan guarantee consortium.

The economic life of Emilia-Romagna – where more than a third of the workforce is self-employed and where *per capita* incomes are the highest in Italy – is based on an accumulation of assumptions about capital and labour, and about the skill and autonomy of the individual worker that are scarcely grasped in our patronising British attitudes towards the needs of small business. Our interest in the Italian economy tends to focus, just as it does in Britain, around the giant multinational corporations whose capital is readily shifted between countries and indeed to new manufacturing bases which are continents away. We see Italy as the vast empire of FIAT and the Agnelli family, or as firms like Benetton. Yet economists, faced with the fact that the Italian economy weathered the storms of the 1970s, attribute it to the buoyancy of the intricate network of very small firms, and 'in 1981, the onset of the recession tested whether the system that had done so well in times of general growth could survive in times of hardship. The network not only survived, but prospered.'[12] In Britain we have come to take it for granted that prosaic consumer goods, like washing machines or refrigerators, or even motor-cycles (of which there are at least six Italian varieties), can only be produced abroad.

I sought explanations from sociologists, economists and workers for these differences. I was told by a British historian that if you compare the experience of car workers in Coventry and Birmingham with those of Turin, a third generation of skilled industrial workers in English factories have been 'moulded in worker-resistance to industrial capitalism'. They know nothing about ways of working except employment for big capitalists, whereas in Turin, with its high 'generation-turnover' of new industrial workers from the south, the artisans and peasants who moved north were not 'crushed by factory capitalism'. They have consequently found it easier to become self-employed workers or employees of small-scale, high-technology entrepreneurs, or to drop out of industrial work almost completely and pick up a living from small-scale horticulture. It is certainly impressive to see how so many people in Italy live in a world which is precisely that of pre-industrial society and is predicted as the likely pattern of post-industrial work: a 'belt-and-braces' combination of several sources of employment for the same individual, built around resourcefulness and adaptability and upon the needs of the season. When I was at Mr Mazzanti's workshop at Trebbo di Reno in the industrial fringe of Bologna, two of his employees had taken time off to gather in the maize harvest (Kropotkin's ideal of the combination of agricultural and industrial work). At the same time, in among the houses around us were small firms involved in steel tube fabrication, thermoplastics, furniture, aerodynamics, leather, enamelling, bottle-making, compressed air, clothing, forge and foundry, precision tools, electronics and ceramics.

Several of the explanations I was given for the differences between Britain and Italy contradict our received wisdom. One was the high degree of autonomy in regional and city governments. Another was that the members of this community of small business and individual initiative were dominantly left-wing voters, supporting a high level of municipal activity. Yet another was the diffusion of entrepreneurial know-how. I questioned two eminent economists who have studied the Italian experience. One was Professor Sebastiano Brusco of Modena University, who stressed that 'Everybody in Emilia has a direct experience of what a firm means, of what it means to apply to a business consultant, to meet with marketing difficulties, to deal with banks and credit institutions, and, above all, how to associate with a friend to start some new activity.' The other was Professor Vittorio Rieser of Turin University, who reflected on those factors about working life that nurture resourcefulness and adaptability. He talked about the wasted creativity involved in assembly-line production – whether in Turin, Detroit, Coventry or Birmingham – which actually found an outlet when people were working for themselves in the post-industrial equivalent of the fine-grain city.

The experience of Italian cities has been thoroughly documented.[13] How does it relate to British efforts to encourage small enterprises? A most significant factor is that of access to credit. It is hard to think of any credit institution in Britain that would provide finance for very advanced machinery to shop-floor workers who did not intend to become large-scale operators. Another is the absence of those informal communication networks so evident in Italy. Yet another is the loss of confidence observable on two levels. One is in government, top management and the stock exchange, where, after years of fruitless subsidy of large-scale industry, it is assumed that products can no longer be made, only services provided. The other, at a shop-floor level, is that the 'likes of us' could never run a productive enterprise. The importance of ventures like the community workshop is that they *could*, locally and among friends, make that leap from production for the household to production for the market. Ventures of that kind can help form the link between the pre-industrial domestic economy and the post-industrial local economy. Professor Ray Pahl, looking at the history of work, suggests that

> The emergence of a polarity between employment and unemployment is in marked contrast to the continuum of mixes of different forms of work typical of earlier times. It may be that in the last years of the twentieth century we are witnessing a return to a world where the continuum is more apposite than a polar dualistic concept. However, those who can do without money to provide goods and services are in a very small minority as ordinary people's alternative means of subsistence have been gradually eroded over the last 200 years.[14]

In the painful transition to the future urban economy, where mass employment gives way to self-directed work, it is worth considering George Benello's conclusion that 'Italy has taught the world perhaps more than any other nation about urban life and urban form. Once again it is in the forefront, creating a new economic order, based on the needs of the city and on human scale.'

CHAPTER 12

GREEN CITIES

Before the explosion in the population in the nineteenth century, cities were green. Old maps show them to be full of gardens both around and detached from the houses. Birmingham was a garden city. A historian of the years 1810–20 celebrated 'the Birmingham working man' with whom 'the cultivation of flowers was carried to great perfection' and in 1825 the author of *A Picture of Birmingham* recorded that

> . . . from the west end of this area (north of the town centre) we enjoy a pleasing and lively summer-view over a considerable tract of land laid out in small gardens. This mode of applying plots of ground in the immediate vicinity of the town, is highly beneficial to the inhabitants . . . They promote healthful exercise and rational enjoyment among families of the artisans; and, with good management, produce an ample supply of those wholesome vegetable stores, which are comparatively seldom tasted by the middling classes when they have to be purchased.[1]

The Georgian square, in both its grand and its humble forms, combining urbanity and greenness, was the finest architectural expression of the domestic love of foliage. Thus even in the most tightly packed streets of terraced houses the view from the rear upstairs window was of plants in pots, barrels, orange-boxes and old tin cans among the wash-houses and privies in tiny backyards. In Nottingham a century ago, when the close-packed terraces often even omitted a backyard, one family in three had an allotment on which they grew roses as well as cabbages. The urban back garden has always been one of the most cherished of amenities, being used not only as an outdoor room, a storage space, a workshop, a dump, a playpen and safe playground, but also as the one place where people can indulge in their passion for growing things. The uses change from family to family and from time to time in the same household. The important thing is that the space is there and that the space is theirs. The managers of urban space ignored these domestic priorities (which, no doubt, they automatically enjoyed themselves). Sir Ashley Bramall wisely commented that the old county of London was a city of small houses, and

> Not only did the war scatter the population and destroy the homes, but it led to the rebuilding of London as a city of blocks of flats, of increasing height. This change has never been fully accepted by the population and there has been an increasing urge for movement to outer London and to the counties beyond, where the old pattern of street and house and garden could be recaptured.[2]

In fact it could always have been recaptured. A variation on the Georgian square developed in some places in the early nineteenth century: the hollow square. Here there was street, house and garden, but the garden opened into, or overlooked, a hidden open space which was surrounded on all four sides by streets, but gave an impression of rural seclusion. They occur not only on a grand scale behind Holland Park and Ladbroke Grove in West London, but also in a more workaday way in Fulham where, in the 1960s, there was still an enclosed smallholding surrounded by the densest pattern of streets, or in Hackney, where the neighbours in surrounding streets have colonised one of these secret gardens to provide allotments and an adventure playground. When I expressed amazement at the great green space beyond the garden of his house in Lansdowne Road, W11, the late Derek Bridgwater told me that every urban pundit from Steen Eiler Rasmussen to Lewis Mumford had been just as surprised. It is almost 80 years since Raymond Unwin demonstrated, in his pamphlet *Nothing Gained by Overcrowding!*,[3] the immense saving in development costs which this layout provided, as well as the advantages for the occupants. Happily, the Mulberry Housing Co-operative, described in Chapter 9, follows precisely the layout of the hollow square. It is a much more useful and usable form of open space than a sea of municipal grass around a housing estate.

But the provision of greenery in the urban environment is not primarily a matter of residential layout, for it depends on easy and daily access. In the nineteenth century, battles were fought to preserve ancient commons for public use, benefactors dedicated parkland to their communities and the city fathers established the tradition of public parks. In the twentieth century, planning standards were laid down to ensure that there was a certain quantity of open space per 1,000 of population. The National Playing Fields Association, which saw its function as broader than the simple provision of football fields or cricket pitches, drew attention to the overcrowded inner city areas which were inevitably under-provided for by comparison with richer or newer parts of the city.[4] Wartime bombing provided the opportunity for local authorities to convert some inner city areas back to grass in attempts to make good the deficiencies in playing field and playground space. Some very dreary and windy open spaces resulted. Official attitudes, as late as the 1960s and 1970s, were

. . . based on a hierarchical principle: parks fulfil different functions with increasing size and distance from the home. Variety of park function is thus achieved through a spatial supply of sites where the most diverse functions are offered by the largest parks. The hierarchy assumes that parks of equivalent status offer the same quality of recreational experiences and that they are equally accessible to all sections of the community.[5]

The shift in perception that contradicted this hierarchical, statistical approach to the provision of green space in the city was a result of the emergence of what is loosely called the 'environmental' movement. This has taken a variety of forms, sometimes with very different aims. One branch is the intense growth of interest in wildlife, where changes in rural life, especially in agriculture, have resulted in the paradox that, like the gypsies, wild creatures can often best be studied in the cities. Old graveyards, railway embankments, reservoirs and derelict sites became a sanctuary for both flora and fauna. This is not a new phenomenon. It was carefully recorded after the war by Robin Fitter[6] and given new topicality by Richard Mabey in the 1970s.[7] By the 1980s it was possible for Bob Smythe, an inner city councillor for five years, to publish a gazetteer of urban wildlife sites in Greater London, Bristol and South Wales, Birmingham and the Midlands, Manchester and the north-west, Yorkshire and the north-east, and Scotland.[8] The fact that he can guide us to over 300 urban wildlife sites is not only an indication of a change in perception, but also of altered professional and official attitudes in response to the incredible spread of local wildlife groups since the 1970s. Such bodies as the British Trust for Conservation Volunteers have moved from being organisers of voluntary activists who are now 'increasingly unhappy at their own diminishing influence on the Trust's affairs' to becoming large-scale employers of labour under the ever-changing regime of urban aid, 'partnership' and EEC funding. They have to exploit the sources of finance available to them, and they simply reflect the enormous interest in the greening of the cities.

Parallel with the urban wildlife movement has been the growth of city farms. We forget how within living memory, not only horses but also cows, sheep, goats, pigs and poultry were kept in inner city areas. 'Much of this husbandry was insanitary, a lot of it was downright cruel, but it is true that before the war, the East End was teeming with animals.'[9] The rediscovery of urban farming began with the initiative of Inter Action in Kentish Town in London in 1972. It has a community workshop, riding school, stable, sheep, goats, pigs, rabbits, geese, chickens, ducks and a cow. There is a conscious aim of mixing age-groups, with children and young people looking after the animals while adults, working on their own projects, are constantly around. A second such venture in the derelict Surrey Docks was the work of Hilary Peters who paradoxically remarked that 'I find farming methods in the country very cruel and difficult to stomach. Farming in London is easier and freer.'[10] The movement spread. I remember from the late 1970s the local couple, who found their ideal mission in running the Spitalfields Farm, reflecting on the educational value of sending children to the market wholesalers to scrounge fodder for the livestock they had come to cherish. The Mudchute in the Isle of Dogs is a hummocky area that originated from the dumping of waste material excavated when the Millwall Docks were first built. This 30-acre site became the biggest of all city farms, with a grant from the London Docklands Development Corporation: 'Look closely, and all of the poignant contradictions of the eighties are here, as cows graze peacefully beneath the tower blocks – the beleaguered local community, the cheerful, and expert, local history group and Community Poster Project.'[11] At the eastern end of the Docklands area, I found the Beckton Meadows Community Small-holding in a two-and-a-half acre wedge of former allotment land where a handful of local people, convinced that animal husbandry is an essential aspect of urban life, keep goats, geese, ducks, rabbits and a breeding sow, with a bunch of children and teenagers to help them. Through accidents of history, the London Residuary Body owns the site and has a statutory duty to make the maximum financial gain from it, when the LDDC is ready to bid.

The city farm movement has spread, not through any official body but from local enthusiasm, to every city in Britain. There are now between 50 and 60 such ventures, linked by a quarterly journal.[12] A similar burst of new interest has arisen in the world of the allotment or community garden. Allotment gardens have been part of the urban scene for 200 years. They have symbolic and historical significance as the only enshrinement in law of the ancient and universal belief that every family has a right of access to land for food production. The legislation does not say where, when or how soon the citizens can have their plots. Some local authorities have waiting lists, others have embarrassingly empty ground. A sharp postwar decline led the government to review policy and recommend legislative and other changes by way of a committee chaired by Professor Harry Thorpe.[13] He saw the allotment movement as declining, an enthusiasm of a dwindling bunch of old men which would die with them unless radical changes were introduced. No government has acted on his recommendations, published in 1969, but his forebodings of inevitable decline did not come true. For, in the 1970s, the new environmental consciousness, ideas of self-sufficiency, and the upsurge of enthusiasm for fresh and organically grown food brought a new influx of demand. It was reported in 1979 that 'Nearly all towns and cities in Great Britain are experiencing a boom in the interest shown in allotments. In England and Wales, the waiting list for allotments has gone up a staggering 1,600 per cent.'[14]

By the 1980s the demand has stabilised and allotment societies are ill-equipped to withstand the pressures on local authorities to dispose of land for more profitable uses, despite the statutory protection. Sometimes these pressures have been successfully resisted but, in any case, a whole series of new initiatives, outside the traditional allotment movement, have sought to make new gardens in the heart of the inner cities. In Moss Side, Manchester, Bill McKeever of Playthorpe Street, through a total personal commitment, has established new allotments in the Housing Action Area. In the East End of Glasgow the Barrowfield Community Association has established its own secret gardens. In Hackney, East London, a local general practitioner, Jon Fuller, has persuaded the council to release and fence a whole series of pocket-sized sites for the New Hackney Allotment Society. In Newcastle upon Tyne the activities co-ordinated by Voluntary Initiatives in Vacant Areas (VIVA) have created a variety of new gardens. In Sparkbrook, Birmingham, the Ashram Asian Vegetable Project has turned abandoned land into food production for the local community. In Islington a group of residents made use of the council's Partnership Programme to make the Culpepper Community Garden.

These initiatives, like dozens of others, are not co-ordinated and, in fact, there is no reason why they should be. For they depend absolutely upon local enthusiasm and energy, and on the ability to make use of the range of grants and special funding, as well as of temporary work funded by the Youth Employment Scheme or the now-abandoned Community Programme. The reliance on short-term funding and job-creation projects brings its own difficulties, but has also enabled local groups to establish new permanent work in city greening and in associated activities, such as recycling waste products, insulating houses and other environmental improvements.[15] The greening of the cities, in thousands of little local projects, is a genuinely popular movement[16] made possible by the thinning-out of the overcrowded industrial city. Yet these values emerging from the daily lives of city dwellers are consistently undervalued by politicians and professions. Jonathon Porritt reports that 'greenery seems to have become irrevocably entangled in the barbed wire of class antagonism by being perceived as being overwhelmingly middle class'.[17] On the other hand, when Jacquelin Burgess and Carolyn Harrison of the geography department of University College, London, attended a conference on public perceptions of the country-side, they reported with dismay that 'Throughout the proceedings the general public was portrayed as insensitive, ignorant and passive; as people who do not share the same insights, knowledge or active concerns of the committed few.'[18]

Doctors Harrison and Burgess were entitled to be dismissive, as for years they had been conducting an extensive series of interviews and group discussions to discover the concepts, beliefs and values about the green environment among residents of different neighbourhoods in several inner city areas ranging from a white working-class district, through a group of Asian women, to a middle-class community.

They found that these groups, regardless of social class, income or residence, 'gained great pleasure from the natural world', less in parks or playing fields than in daily life. The sensuous experience of encountering the natural world gave enormous pleasure in 'walks along the riverside', round the houses and on the way to school; waste places seen from the top of a bus or used by children; streams and scrubby bits; farmland, woodland, golf courses, cemeteries and squares in shopping centres. All these spaces, especially 'the wild bits', and most especially among people living in estates without gardens, were highly valued because they provide places 'where children can have adventures, experience independence for the first time, enjoy the companionship of other children, and discover the natural world'.

This view of the social role of the urban green was given great stress by the Asian women, 'separated from their childhood by geographical distance as well as age', and whose ordinary experiences of open spaces include racial abuse and physical harassment. Indeed, since everyday fears, especially of more wooded and secluded places, include assault and violence, sexual dangers for women and children, vandalism, glue-sniffing and every kind of contemporary horror, Doctors Harrison and Burgess stress the need for more *social* management of these places which have a *social* meaning.[19]

They tried to find a concept that really reflected the aspirations of the inner city groups whose green values they explored, which embraced the sensory experience of contact with nature, the wonderland of adventurous play for the young, and a shared experience with children, families, neighbours and friends. The memorable phrase which occurred to them was outside the vocabulary of the parks department, the director of leisure services and even, I fear, that of the conservation lobby. It was 'gateways to a better world'.

CHAPTER 13

A CHECKLIST FOR CITIZENS

If there were obvious and universal solutions to the problems of the inner cities they would have been discovered years ago. I suspect that for many people the very phrase 'inner city' is simply a euphemism for other issues: those of racial prejudice, or those of crime or the drug traffic. The more we amalgamate different social issues together under this general label, the less likely we are to be able to cope with any of them separately. For me, the words refer to the poor minority of inner city dwellers and I deplore the fact that current policies ignore its existence and consequently ignore the smouldering resentment building up in the cities. I want to recommend to fellow-citizens of all parties or of none, a handful of ideas expressed in terms intended to win the widest possible support.

1 Do Something about Land Valuation

The first is that whatever fiscal benefits accrue as a result of the property boom and property speculation, the effect on poor city dwellers is to destroy any opportunity they might have to do anything for themselves. This question of land valuation is a very old issue in British politics and the fact that it has slipped off the political agenda does not reduce its importance. Before the First World War, the government was on the brink of introducing the taxation of site values. After the Second World War, the Planning Act of 1947 introduced the nationalisation of the development value of land, later rescinded. Subsequent governments in the 1960s and 1970s established the Land Commission and the Community Land Act, in ever more complicated legislation to achieve the same result. Both were abandoned by later governments. But in the absence of the political will and foresight needed to recoup for the community the

development value of sites which have become too 'valuable' for
socially useful purposes, we are left with two strategies. These are that
either the planning machinery must be used to depress hypothetical
values by designating land for uses less profitable than those assumed
by the district valuer, or the public purse must bear the cost of
artificially depressing site values for specific purposes. This is not a
hypothetical or academic issue. The only reason why the redevelopment of the Coin Street area of the South Bank in London (see
Chapter 9) was possible was that the site was designated as 'fair rent'
housing. The reason why existing small firms are still being driven out
of the Docklands area (see Chapter 6) is simply a matter of site
valuation. The reason why the William Curtis Ecological Park,
opposite the Tower of London in the ancient Bermondsey dock,
closed in 1985 – after eight years and 100,000 visitors – was because
this symbol of 'the greening of the city' was less 'valuable' than the
office complex that replaced it. But how many citizens would miss the
offices, compared to those who miss the park?

2 Help People House Themselves, Inside and Outside the City

The second point is closely related. The real shining lights of urban
regeneration in Britain in the last decade are the range of tiny
initiatives for dweller-controlled rehousing (see Chapter 10), whether
in the form of tenant co-operatives or of self-build housing
associations, whose financial viability depends on a network of local
professional and advisory resources to get them off the ground. This
does not apply only to the cities. Mechanisms have to be devised to
enable low-income people to join everyone else in the general
dispersal of settlement patterns that has been evident throughout this
century. The escalation of site values *outside* the cities has made this
kind of movement, taken absolutely for granted by everyone above a
certain income level, impossible for the poor (see Chapter 4). It also
prevents people without work in northern cities from being able to
accept vacant jobs in the south.

3 Give Real Encouragement to Small Enterprise

The third point is similarly linked with site values and consequently
with rental values. Our belated discovery of small business should

persuade us to learn from the Italian example and to realise that, as well as a supportive political and organisational environment, it has depended on two things: low overheads and access to credit. Yet site valuation and high interest rates are still eliminating small businesses in Britain. Britain has 2.5 million self-employed people. Italy, with a similar total population, has 7.5 million as a result, among other things, of a policy agreed between the political right and left, of positive support, cheap credit, advice and market intelligence, and pooled accountancy and financial services, as well as the availability of sites and premises. The social benefits are enormous.

4   Make the Cities Green Again

The fourth point relates to the inner city environment. The political debate on public services has never quite reached the point when the decision is made that there should be an admission charge for the use of public parks. The greening of the city, however, is an issue that is advancing steadily forward in the urban agenda. At last, population movements have enabled us to re-create within the cities the kind of environment that people leave the cities to find, and which was normal before the industrial revolution packed the cities with the new urban proletariat. Glasgow was once a 'good green place' and is slowly becoming one again. A deep groundswell of opinion is not only yearning for back gardens, but also for playspace, city farms, allotments, city nature reserves and urban wild places. We can seize the opportunities, or we can ignore this demand as sentimental or irrelevant, claiming once again that city land is much too precious to be devoted to the expressed needs of the citizens.

5   Find New Ways of Engaging the Young

My fifth point is about schooling. Contemporary youth culture is profoundly hostile to, and suspicious of, the education system. In those parts of the country where there is a reasonable hope of work or of further education leading to work, other influences are operating on the young. In the local culture of the inner city these other influences are weakened or absent, and young people from ethnic minorities have the completely justified conviction that they are victimised by racial discrimination. A dozen publicly funded projects, from the Education Priority Areas of the 1960s to the current promotion of 'compacts' between schools and employers, have sought to enhance the perceived value of schooling for children in places that are seen as 'deprived'. Such special efforts are always justified, even though their results are hard to measure because of the time-lag before we can assess whether or not they have produced successful citizens. They are also the first items to be cut when educational spending is reduced.

The likeliest successes, among the people where it matters most, are those ventures outside the school system that try to change young people's lives by introducing new skills and attainments: all those attempts at providing them with computer skills (rejected at school), or at turning those convicted of taking-and-driving-away into car mechanics or stock-car racers. They cannot be planned for because they depend on special individuals outside the official payroll. They are expensive, precisely because they are labour-intensive. But they are the areas where the widespread belief that 'something should be done about inner city kids' is most likely to reach the ones who have rejected school. What should we do with this tiresome 15-year-old truant? The answer is to give him or her a *paid* job in a pre-school playgroup and open up career prospects.

Purchasing power is a much appreciated commodity, especially for those who lack it. Every city has huge tasks of social and environmental maintenance which are not being undertaken and which would be made attractive by the prospect of a pay-packet at the end of the week.

6 Give Access to Tools and Technology

A sixth point, linked in several ways with the others, is the idea of the community workshop (see Chapter 11), where people have access to machinery, work-space and advice, in order to meet their own needs and do their own thing. The idea has been around for years and has had a new impetus because of mass unemployment. The Manpower Services Commission Community Programme funded several of these but, of course, funding was cut off with the demise of the programme. This is absurd, and so is the usual stipulation that nothing should be done in the workshop that would provide a monetary gain for the user. The community workshop is an idea that should be expanded and enlarged into a base for enterprise. It should be a skill-exchange and an alternative to school for the young; a sheltered workshop for the infirm as well as a starting pad for those who want to be independent but do not know how.

7 Change the Terms of the Debate

Finally, I find it appalling that our prescriptions for the future of the cities are framed in a sterile debate on the virtues of public or private enterprise and a sanctimonious advocacy of partnership between the two. The ordinary daily needs of poor city dwellers are ignored in this clash of ideologies, whether they are for locally accessible work, decent housing, cheap public transport or schooling that really engages their children. This has nothing to do with the physical constraints of the city: the Civic Trust Survey of Urban Wasteland calculates that there is enough empty land in the cities to accommodate another city the size of Leeds. I have looked in vain for an explanation of this abdication of civic responsibility, which would have seemed appalling to any urban politician of any party a century ago. The most relevant explanation I have found comes from David Donnison and Alan Middleton in their study of Glasgow.[1] They comment that

> In the absence of any strong tradition of social solidarity, governments survive by keeping large and powerful groups happy and excluding those whose needs can be most easily disregarded. Glasgow's east end is one of the places where the trick is worked (middle class people, we found, hardly ever go there, and those of them who work there do not live there). The poor are the powerless — the people who can most easily be excluded without political turbulence from the opportunities available to the average skilled and prosperous worker. Thus policies for helping deprived people and deprived areas which do not address their powerlessness are unlikely to make a lasting impact because they are not dealing with the fundamental issue.

I see very few signs of a change of heart or mind. But before we begin to count the huge cost of enabling thousands of modest, sensible ventures to get off the ground in the inner city, let us consider the enormous expenditure we have incurred over the past 40 years in pursuing grand strategies that have not worked for inner city dwellers and have all too often done them positive harm.

Notes

Introduction

1 Ted Robert Gurr and Desmond S. King, *The State and the City* (Macmillan, 1987).
2 Barry Knight, 'Out of the Fire: A Stateside View of Britain's Inner Cities' (unpublished paper from the Centre for Research and Innovation in Social Policy and Practice, 1988).
3 See Peter Hall, *Cities of Tomorrow* (Basil Blackwell, 1988).
4 Patrick Geddes, *Town Planning towards City Development: A Report Prepared for the Durbar of Indore, India*, vol. 1 (1918).
5 See Peter Hall, *London 2001* (Unwin Hyman, 1988).
6 John F. C. Turner, *Housing by People: Towards Autonomy in Building Environments* (Marion Boyars, 1976).

1 The Elusive Golden Age

1 Peter Hall (ed.), *The Inner City in Context: Final Report of the Social Science Research Council Inner Cities Working Party* (Heinemann, 1981).
2 S. G. Checkland, *The Upas Tree: Glasgow 1875–1975*, 2nd edn (University of Glasgow Press, 1981).
3 Alan Middleton, 'Glasgow and its East End', in David Donnison and Alan Middleton (eds), *Regenerating the Inner City: Glasgow's Experience* (Routledge & Kegan Paul, 1987).
4 Cited by Ian Adams in *The Making of Urban Scotland* (Croom Helm, 1978).
5 Malcolm MacEwen, *Architecture in Crisis* (RIBA, 1976).
6 R. E. C. Lond in *The Fortnightly Review* (January 1903), quoted by T. C. Smout in *A Century of the Scottish People 1830–1950* (Collins, 1986).

7 Asa Briggs, *Victorian Cities* (Pelican, 1968).
8 Anthony Wohl, *Endangered Lives: Public Health in Victorian Britain* (Dent, 1983).
9 Bill Luckin, *Pollution and Control: A Social History of the Thames in the 19th century* (Adam Hilger, 1986).
10 Peter Hall 'Postscript', in Anthony Sutcliffe (ed.), *Metropolis 1890–1940* (Mansell, 1984).
11 Peter Hall and Dennis Hay, *Growth Centres in the European Urban System* (Heinemann Educational, 1981).
12 William J. Fishman, *East End 1881: A Year in a London Borough among the Labouring Poor* (Duckworth, 1988).
13 Hall (ed.), *The Inner City in Context*.

2 After the Urban Explosion

1 Peter Hall, *Cities of Tomorrow* (Basil Blackwell, 1988).
2 Steve Platt, 'Planning the anarchist way', *New Statesman and Society*, 13 January 1989.
3 William Morris, *News from Nowhere* (originally published 1891; Routledge & Kegan Paul, 1970, 1983).
4 Philip Boardman, *The Worlds of Patrick Geddes* (Routledge & Kegan Paul, 1978). See also Paddy Kitchen, *A Most Unsettling Person* (Gollancz, 1975) and Patrick Geddes, *Cities in Evolution: An Introduction to the Town Planning Movement and to the Study of Civics* (originally published 1915; Williams & Norgate, 1949, Ernest Benn, 1968).
5 Peter Kropotkin, *Fields, Factories and Workshops* (originally published 1898; Freedom Press, 1985).
6 Lewis Mumford, *The City in History* (Seeker & Warburg, 1961).
7 Ebenezer Howard, opening the discussion of a paper on 'Civics as Applied Sociology' by Patrick Geddes, read at a meeting in the London School of Economics, 18 July 1904, reprinted in Helen Mellor (ed.), *The Ideal City* (Leicester University Press, 1979).
8 Ebenezer Howard, *Garden Cities of Tomorrow* (originally published 1898; Faber, 1946, 1970, 1983).
9 Frederic Osborn, *Green-Belt Cities*, 2nd edn (Evelyn, Adams & MacKay, 1969).
10 Frederick Osborn and Arnold Whittick, *New Towns. Their Origins, Achievements and Progress* (Routledge & Kegan Paul, 1977).
11 Hazel Evans (ed.), *New Towns: The British Experience* (Charles Knight, 1972).

12 David Hall, *Without the Inner City* (Third Norman Wall Memorial Lecture, Midland New Towns Society, 1977).
13 Town and Country Planning Association, *Whose Responsibility? Reclaiming the Inner Cities* (TCPA, April 1986).
14 Martin Boddy, John Lovering and Keith Bassett, *Sunbelt City? A Study of Economic Change in Britain's M4 Growth Corridor* (Clarendon Press, 1986).
15 Robert Chesshyre, *The Return of a Native Reporter* (Viking Press, 1987)
16 Howard, *Garden Cities of Tomorrow.*

3 Death of the Fine-Grain City

1 J. W. R. Whitehand, *Rebuilding Town Centres: Developers, Architects and Styles* (University of Birmingham Dept. of Geography, Occasional Publication no. 19, 1984).
2 Sam Bass Warner, *Streetcar Suburbs: The Process of Growth in Boston (1870–1900)* (Cambridge, Mass. : Harvard University Press, 1962).
3 James Finlayson, *Urban Devastation: The Planning of Incarceration* (Solidarity Press, 1976).
4 Jaqueline Tyrwhitt (ed.), *Patrick Geddes in India* (Lund Humphries, 1947).
5 Quoted by Asa Briggs in *Victorian Cities* (Pelican, 1968).
6 Sir Herbert Manzoni, speaking at the Royal Institute of British Architects, March 1958.
7 Association for Urban Quality, *The Way to a Better Bull Ring* (A report with recommendations to city councillors) (Birmingham, March 1988).
8 Ibid. Italics in original.
9 Richard Tomkins 'Planners redesign second city's centre', *Financial Times*, 21 October 1988.
10 'Bull Ring piazza gives human touch', *Architects' Journal*, vol. 188, no. 45 (November 1988).
11 See, for example, *Furnishing the World: The East London Furniture Trade 1830–1980* (Journeyman Press, 1987).
12 Andrew Gibb, *Glasgow: The Making of a City* (Croom Helm, 1983).
13 Nick Wates, *The Battle for Tolmers Square* (Routledge & Kegan Paul, 1976).
14 Peter Ambrose and Bob Colenutt, *The Property Machine* (Penguin, 1975).

15 Deirdre Mason, 'The Catch 22 of city regeneration', *The Surveyor*, 28 January 1988.

4 Trapped in the City

1 This claim is presented in detail in Colin Ward, *Tenants Take Over* (Architectural Press, 1974).
2 Martin J. Elson, *Green Belts: Conflict Mediation in the Urban Fringe* (Heinemann, 1986).
3 Lewis Keeble, review in *The Planner* (Journal of the Royal Town Planning Institute), vol. 72, no. 6 (June 1986).
4 Graeme Shankland, Peter Willmott and David Jordan, *Inner London: Policies for Dispersal and Balance* (HMSO, 1977).
5 N. Buck, I. Gordon and K. Young, *The London Employment Problem* (ESRC Inner Cities Research Programme Series, Clarendon Press, 1986).
6 Maurice Ash, *New Renaissance* (Green Books, 1987).
7 Tim Mars, personal communication to the author, reporting interviews in 'Diverse Reports', Channel 4 TV, 11 June 1986.
8 Anthony King, *The Bungalow: The Production of a Global Culture* (Routledge & Kegan Paul, 1984).
9 Dennis Hardy and Colin Ward, *Arcadia for All: The Legacy of a Makeshift Landscape* (Mansell, 1984).
10 Colin Ward, 'The Do-it-Yourself New Town'. Paper given at the Garden Cities/New Towns Forum, Welwyn Garden City, 22 October 1975, partly printed in *Town and Country Planning*, May 1976, *The Municipal Review*, May 1976, and *Undercurrents*, June–July 1976.
11 Town and Country Planning Association, *A Third Garden City: Outline Prospectus* (TCPA, 1979).
12 Andrew Wood, *Greentown: A Case Study of a Proposed Alternative Community* (Open University Energy and Environment Research Unit, 1988).
13 Tony Gibson, *Counterweight: The Neighbourhood Option* (TCPA and Education for Neighbourhood Change, 1984).
14 'New Garden Cities: The solution to the problems of the southeast', *The Planner*, June 1988.
15 Ferdinand Mount, 'Doing something about poverty', *Spectator*, 11 July 1987.
16 Stephen Holley, letter to the editor of *Town and Country Planning*, May 1977.

5 Bringing in the Task Force

1 R. E. Pahl, summing up the 'Save Our Cities' Conference, sponsored by the *Sunday Times* and the Gulbenkian Foundation, Bristol 1976.

2 Derek Fraser and Anthony Sutcliffe, Introduction to Fraser and Sutcliffe (eds), *The Pursuit of Urban History* (Edward Arnold, 1983).

3 T. Dan Smith, *An Autobiography* (Oriel Press, 1970).

4 Wilfred Burns, *New Towns for Old* (Leonard Hill, 1963).

5 Ibid.

6 Alison Ravetz, *Remaking Cities* (Croom Helm, 1983).

7 Sir Wilfred Burns, addressing the seminar of the Artist Placement Group, Royal College of Art, 1978.

8 Some of the CDP reports from the 1970s can still be obtained from the Planning Bookshop, 17 Carlton House Terrace, London SW1Y 5AH. Their titles, which reflect their general approach, include *Local Government Becomes Big Business* (1976), *Profits against Houses* (1976), *Whatever Happened to Council Housing?* (1976), *Gilding the Ghetto* (1977), and *Working Class Politics and Housing* (1978).

9 Indian Workers' Association, *The Regeneration of Racism: Hypocrisy of Inner City Policies* (IWA, 1987). Available from 112a The Green, Southall UB2 4BQ.

10 Ted Robert Gurr and Desmond S. King, *The State and the City* (Macmillan, 1987).

11 Lord Scarman (the Scarman Report), *The Brixton Disorders 10–12 April 1981* (Penguin, 1982).

12 Gurr and King, *The State and the City*.

13 Ibid.

14 Murray Stewart, 'Ten years of inner cities policy', *Town Planning Review*, vol. 58, no. 2 (April 1987).

15 Gideon Ben-Tovim, 'Race, politics and urban regeneration: lessons from Liverpool', in Michael Parkinson, Bernard Foley and Dennis Judd (eds), *Regenerating the Cities: The UK Crisis and the US Experience* (Manchester University Press and the Fulbright Commission, 1988).

16 Stewart, 'Ten years of inner cities policy'.

17 Yvonne Roberts, 'Boys with the greenbacks', *New Statesman and Society*, 9 December 1988.

18 Ibid.

19 Stewart, 'Ten years of inner cities policy'. See also Charles

Landry, Dave Morley, Russell Southwood and Patrick Wright, *What a Way to Run a Railroad* (Comedia, 1985).
20 Department of the Environment, *Policy for the Inner Cities* (HMSO, 1977).
21 *Faith in the City: A Call for Action by Church and Nation.* Report of the Archbishop of Canterbury's Commission on Urban Priority Areas (Church House Publishing, 1985).
22 Town and Country Planning Association, *Whose Responsibility? Reclaiming the Inner Cities* (TCPA, April 1986).
23 Ibid.

6 Tales of Two Cities

1 David Donnison and Alan Middleton (eds), *Regenerating the Inner City: Glasgow's Experience* (Routledge & Kegan Paul, 1987).
2 Dennis Hardy, *Making Sense of the London Docklands: Processes of Change* (Middlesex Polytechnic, Geography and Planning Paper no. 9, October 1983).
3 Ibid.
4 Town and Country Planning Association, *Whose Responsibility? Reclaiming the Inner Cities* (TCPA, April 1986).
5 Cited in Donnison and Middleton, *Regenerating the Inner City.*
6 E. Gillett, *Investment in the Environment* (Aberdeen University Press, 1983).
7 Donnison and Middleton, *Regenerating the Inner City.*
8 David Clapham and Keith Kintrea, 'Public housing', in Donnison and Middleton, *Regenerating the Inner City.*
9 Ibid.
10 Shiela T. McDonald, 'Some environmental considerations', in Donnison and Middleton, *Regenerating the Inner City.*
11 Interviewed by Martyn Halsall in 'Revival of grassroots lifts Scots', *Guardian*, 7 November 1988.
12 Hardy, *Making Sense of the London Docklands.*
13 Ibid.
14 London Docklands Study Team, *Docklands Redevelopment Proposals for East London* (1983).
15 Hardy, *Making Sense of the London Docklands.*
16 Local Government Planning and Land Act 1980, Part XVI.
17 House of Commons Employment Committee, Third Report, *The Employment Effects of Urban Development Corporations* (HMSO, 1988).

18 Ibid.
19 Nick Wates and Charles Knevitt, *Community Architecture* (Penguin, 1977).
20 Harold Jackson, 'Canary Row', *Guardian*, 12 November 1985.
21 Letter from Michael Barraclough to the London Docklands Development Corporation, 14 January 1988.
22 Docklands Consultative Committee, *Urban Development Corporations: Six Years in London's Docklands* (DCC, Unit 4, 4 Romford Road, London E15 4EA, 1988).
23 *Financial Times*, 4 December 1987.
24 House of Commons Employment Committee, op. cit at note 17.

7 Victims of Success: The American Warning

1 See Stuart Butler and Anna Kondratas, *Out of the Poverty Trap: A Conservative Strategy for Welfare Reform* (New York: The Free Press, 1987).
2 The first and second Mount Laurel decisions are reported in 'Opening the suburbs: New Jersey's Mount Laurel experience', *Shelterforce* (publication of the National Housing Institute, USA), vol. 11, no. 2 (August/September 1988).
3 Prince Charles, speaking as chairman of the joint AIA/RIBA Conference on Remaking Cities, Benedum Theatre, Pittsburgh, 5 March 1988.
4 Interviewed in *The Independent*, 4 January 1988.
5 Jim Barber, 'Homeless march in Atlanta, berate candidates', *New Pittsburgh Courier*, 2 March 1988.
6 Barbara Vobejda, 'Atlanta students learn self-esteem: 'street academy' reaches out', *Washington Post*, 14 March 1988.
7 Ronald Smothers, 'Raising the roof to aid the homeless', *Atlanta Journal*, 13 March 1988.
8 Professor Melvin King of MIT, as reported in *The Boston Globe*, 16 November 1987.
9 Documented in Ted Robert Gurr and Desmond S. King, *The State and the City* (Macmillan, 1987).
10 *The Independent*, 4 January 1988.
11 Grady Clay, *Right before Your Eyes: Penetrating the Urban Environment* (Chicago: The Planners Press, 1988).
12 Ibid.
13 Gurr and King, *The State and the City*.
14 See Edmund R. Bacon, 'The language of cities', *Town Planning Review*, vol. 56, no. 2 (April 1985).

15 Butler and Kondratas, *Out of the Poverty Trap.*

8 Stock and Flow in the City Underclass

1 C. R. Martin, *Slums and Slummers: A Sociological Treatise on the Housing Problem* (1935), cited by Michael Hebbert in *The Inner City Problem in Historical Context* (Social Science Research Council, 1980).
2 Sir Keith Joseph, speech at Birmingham, 19 October 1974.
3 John Macnicol, 'In pursuit of the underclass', *Journal of Social Policy*, vol. 16, no. 3 (1987).
4 Charles Dickens, *Uncollected Writings from 'Household Words'*, vol. 1 (Allen Lane, 1972).
5 Oscar Lewis, 'The culture of poverty', *Scientific American*, October 1966.
6 Peter Hall, *Cities of Tomorrow* (Basil Blackwell, 1988).
7 William Julius Wilson, *The Truly Disadvantaged: The Inner City, the Underclass, and Public Policy* (University of Chicago Press, 1987).
8 Alexandra Artley, 'The poor of London', *Spectator*, 13 December 1986.
9 Chris Webb, 'News from Notting Dale', *Bulletin of Environmental Education*, vol. 8, no. 10 (November 1978).
10 Barbara Tizard *et al., Young Children at School in the Inner City* (Lawrence Erlbaum Associates, 1988).

9 The Battle for Coin Street

1 V. S. Pritchett, *London Perceived*, 2nd edn (Chatto & Windus, 1974).
2 Ibid.
3 Steve Barran, in *Coin Street News*, April 1983.
4 Inspector's Report, 10 January 1983 (DoE Decision Letter Ref: GLP/5023/1000/5).
5 Tim Roberts, 'How David took on Goliath and won', *Guardian*, 31 May 1986.
6 Charles Pearson (1855), quoted in Francis Sheppard, *London 1808–1870: The Infernal Wen* (Secker & Warburg 1971).
7 See Robert Sinclair, *Metropolitan Man* (Allen & Unwin, 1938) and John Hewetson, *Ill-Health, Poverty and the State* (Freedom Press, 1946).

8 Michael Hughes (ed.), *The Letters of Lewis Mumford and Frederic J. Osborn* (Adams & Dart, 1971).

9 Graham Lomas, *The Inner City* (London Council of Social Service, 1975).

10 Anne Power, *Property before People: The Management of Twentieth-century Council Housing* (Allen & Unwin, 1987).

11 Colin Ward, *Tenants Take Over* (Architectural Press, 1974).

10 City People *Can* House Themselves

1 Frances McCall at the Building Communities Conference, quoted in Jim Sneddon and Caroline Theobald (eds), *Building Communities* (Community Architecture Information Services, 1987).

2 Jane Morton, 'Glasgow's socialist co-ops', *New Society*, 10 May 1984.

3 Johnston Birchall, *Building Communities: The Co-operative Way* (Routledge & Kegan Paul, 1988).

4 Nick Wates, 'The Liverpool breakthrough: or public sector housing phase 2', *Architects' Journal*, vol. 176, no. 36 (September 1982).

5 Alan McDonald, *The Weller Way* (Faber, 1986).

6 Hugh Anderson, 'Co-op dividends', *Architects' Journal*, vol. 180, no. 29 (July 1984).

7 Tony McGann at the Building Communities Conference, quoted in Sneddon and Theobald (eds), *Building Communities*.

8 Mike Franks, 'Liverpool: resuscitation or decline?', *Built Environment*, March 1975.

9 Colin Ward, 'The leavings of Liverpool', *Town and Country Planning*, October 1976.

10 Abdul Bahar, in *Self Build: A Manual for Self Build Housing Associations* (National Federation of Housing Associations, 1988).

11 See Danny Levine, *Building Young Lives! A Study into the Feasibility of Self-Help Housing for Young Homeless People* (National Federation of Housing Associations, 1989).

12 For example, the Association of Community Technical Aid Centres, Royal Institution, Colquitt Street, Liverpool L1 4DE, and the National Federation of Housing Associations, 175 Gray's Inn Road, London WC1X 8UP.

13 John McKean, *Learning from Segal* (Basle: Birkhäuser Verlag, 1989).

14 Ibid.

15 Brian Richardson, 'Architecture for all', *The Raven*, October 1988. The address of the Walter Segal Self Build Trust is PO Box 542, London SE1 1TX.

11 Can They Make Jobs Too? The Italian Lesson

1 Peter Hall, *London 2001* (Unwin Hyman, 1988).
2 Ivan Turok, 'Continuity, change and contradiction in urban policy', in David Donnison and Alan Middleton (eds), *Regenerating the Inner City: Glasgow's Experience* (Routledge & Kegan Paul, 1987).
3 David Nicholson-Lord, *The Greening of the Cities* (Routledge & Kegan Paul, 1987).
4 *Report of the Committee of Enquiry on Small Firms* (The Bolton Report), Cmnd. 4811 (HMSO, 1971).
5 David Watkins, John Stanworth and Ava Westrip, *Stimulating Small Firms* (Gower, 1982).
6 Cited by Howard Erlich, *Urban Removal* (Baltimore Great Atlantic Radio Conspiracy, 1978).
7 Lewis Mumford, *The City in History* (Secker & Warburg, 1961).
8 Michael J. Piore and Charles F. Sabel, *The Second Industrial Divide* (New York: Basic Books, 1984).
9 Fergus Murray, 'The decentralisation of production – the decline of the mass-collective worker', in R. E. Pahl (ed.), *On Work: Historical, Comparative and Theoretical Approaches* (Basil Blackwell, 1988).
10 C. Richard Hatch, 'Italy's industrial renaissance: are American cities ready to learn?', *Urban Land*, January 1985.
11 Len Krimerman, 'C. George Benello: architect of liberating work', *Changing Work*, no. 7 (Winter 1988).
12 Robert E. Friedman, 'Flexible manufacturing networks', *Entrepreneurial Economy*, vol. 6, no. 1 (July/August 1987).
13 Sebastiano Brusco, 'The Emilian model: productive decentralisation and social integration', *Cambridge Journal of Economics* (June 1982) and Sebastiano Brusco, 'Small firms and industrial districts: the experience of Italy', in David Keeble and Egbert Wever (eds), *New Firms and Regional Development in Europe* (Croom Helm, 1988).
14 R. E. Pahl, Introduction to Pahl (ed.), *On Work*.

12 Green Cities

1 James Drake, *A Picture of Birmingham*, cited in D. Crouch and C. Ward, *The Allotment: Its Landscape and Culture* (Faber, 1988).
2 Ashley Bramall, in *Education*, 3 December 1976.
3 Raymond Unwin, *Nothing Gained by Overcrowding!* (Garden Cities and Town Planning Association, 1912). This rare pamphlet is partly reprinted in Walter Creese (ed.), *The Legacy of Raymond Unwin: A Human Pattern for Planning* (Cambridge, Mass.: MIT Press, 1967). Its key argument is illustrated in Peter Hall, *Cities of Tomorrow* (Basil Blackwell, 1988).
4 Peter Heseltine and John Holborn, *Playgrounds: The Planning, Design and Construction of Play Environments* (Mitchell Publishing, 1987).
5 Jacquelin Burgess, Carolyn Harrison and Melanie Limb, 'People, parks and the urban green: a study of popular meanings and values for open spaces in the city', *Urban Studies*, vol. 25 (1988).
6 R. S. R. Fitter, *London's Natural History* (Collins, 1945).
7 Richard Mabey, *The Unofficial Countryside* (Collins, 1973).
8 Bob Smythe, *City Wildscape* (Hilary Shipman, 1987).
9 Nigel Winfield, interviewed in William Hatchett, 'The greening of the cities', *New Society*, 11 July 1986.
10 Hilary Peters, *Docklandscape* (Watkins, 1979).
11 Hatchett, 'The greening of the cities'.
12 *City Farmer*, published from The Old Vicarage, 66 Fraser Street, Bedminster, Bristol BS3 4LY.
13 *Report of the Departmental Committee of Inquiry into Allotments*, Cmnd. 4166 (HMSO, 1969).
14 Pete Riley, *Economic Growth: The Allotments Campaign Guide* (Friends of the Earth, 1979). For subsequent history see Crouch and Ward, *The Allotment*.
15 Joan Davidson, *How Green Is Your City?* (Bedford Square Press, 1988).
16 David Nicholson-Lord, *The Greening of the Cities* (Routledge & Kegan Paul, 1987).
17 Jonathon Porritt, *The Coming of the Greens* (Fontana, 1988).
18 Jacquelin Burgess and Carolyn Harrison, 'Qualitative research and open space policy', *The Planner* (Journal of the Royal Town Planning Institute), vol. 74, no. 11 (November 1988).
19 Ibid. and Carolyn Harrison, Melanie Limb and Jacquelin Burgess, 'Nature in the city – popular values for a living world', *Journal of Environmental Management*, vol. 25 (1987).

13 A Checklist for Citizens

1 David Donnison and Alan Middleton, *Regenerating the Inner City* (Routledge, 1987).

Index

This item is to be

stan